WEALTH MAXIMISATION THROUGH SMART FINANCIAL LITERACY

GUBIR SINGH KHERA

INDIA • SINGAPORE • MALAYSIA

ISBN 979-8-89446-382-7

Contents

Chapter 1

The Art of Money Mastery

Imagine standing at the edge of a vast financial wilderness. It's wild, unpredictable, and intimidating. Now, picture having a map in your hand, a compass in your pocket, and a clear path marked out before you. This is what financial literacy offers you: a way to figure out your way through this wilderness with confidence and clarity.

Why does this matter, you might wonder? Because at its heart, understanding personal finance is about securing your independence and ensuring your safety in a world where economic winds shift rapidly. It's about being able to make choices that align with your dreams and values, not just your immediate needs.

With economic volatility becoming more pronounced—exemplified by the COVID-19 pandemic's impact on global markets—understanding how to manage personal finances has never been more crucial. A 2020 survey by the National Foundation for Credit Counseling (NFCC) highlighted that 78% of adults wished they had more information available to them about personal finances, indicating a widespread recognition of financial literacy's value.

In an era where economic uncertainties have become the norm, the importance of being financially literate cannot be overstated. It's the difference between living paycheck to paycheck and achieving financial independence. It's the difference between feeling overwhelmed by every financial hiccup and navigating challenges with confidence.

Why Financial Literacy Matters More Than Ever

Independence and Security: Understanding personal finance is foundational to living a life that's not dictated by financial stress but driven by choice and freedom. It's about creating a buffer that can protect you and your family from the unexpected twists and turns of life.

Making Informed Decisions: With the advent of digital banking, cryptocurrencies, and online investment platforms, the financial landscape is evolving at an unprecedented pace. The volume of digital transactions in India, as reported by the Reserve Bank of India, saw a 55% increase in 2020-2021, signaling a shift towards digital finance. This revolution brings both opportunities and risks. Financial literacy empowers you to sift through these options and make decisions that align with your long-term goals.

Avoiding Debt Traps: In a world where credit is easily accessible, it's all too easy to fall into debt traps. Financial literacy provides the knowledge to use credit wisely, avoiding pitfalls that can lead to stressful, debt-ridden situations.

Back when I first started exploring the huge world of finance, where numbers and dollars seem to whisper secrets, I came across a super simple tool that ended up being a game-changer for me: a personal finance journal. This turned into my trusty compass for finding my way through the tricky world of personal finance, which I was diving into both as a professor and as someone super keen to learn all about it.

Starting with a Personal Finance Journal

The revelation came not in a classroom, but in the quiet moments of reflection and recording. I realized that to truly grasp the essence of financial literacy, one must start by understanding their own financial heartbeat—their spending, saving, and investing patterns.

Track Your Spending: I remember stumbling across a statistic from the Centre for Monitoring Indian Economy (CMIE) highlighting the significant fluctuation in household savings rates. This mirrored my own erratic spending habits. By meticulously jotting down every purchase, no matter how small, I began to see the nature of my financial habits. Patterns emerged, some good, some begging for change. This was about setting the stage for mindful financial decisions.

Goal Setting and Review: The World Bank's Global Findex Database served as a stark reminder that only a fraction of adults in India had concrete savings goals. This struck a chord. Without goals, we're sailing without a destination. My journal morphed into a sanctuary where dreams and numbers met—setting financial goals became a ritual, not just a task. Revisiting these goals in the journal kept me tethered to my financial aspirations, making adjustments more meaningful.

Reflect on Money Mindset: Early on, I learned that our financial decisions are deeply rooted in our perceptions and beliefs about money. The journal offered a mirror to my money mindset, challenging me to confront and reshape beliefs that were hindering my financial growth. It was a transformative process, turning obstacles into stepping stones toward financial freedom.

Celebrate Progress: Perhaps the most rewarding aspect of maintaining a finance journal was the opportunity to celebrate every small victory. Each entry marked a step forward, a reminder that progress, no matter how incremental, is still progress. It was here, in the pages of my journal, that I learned the importance of recognizing and celebrating each achievement, fueling my motivation to continue on this path.

This personal finance journal, a humble yet powerful tool, laid the foundation for a journey of continuous learning and improvement. It was my starting point, my 101 in the school of financial literacy, teaching me lessons that would last a lifetime.

Now, let's delve deeper into the core concepts of financial literacy that everyone should grasp. Understanding these foundational principles is like acquiring the keys to unlock your financial potential. It's not just about learning; it's about applying this knowledge to create a secure and prosperous future for yourself.

Core Concepts Everyone Should Know

The Difference Between Assets and Liabilities

Assets are essentially what you own that has value—savings accounts, investments, real estate, and personal property like your car. Liabilities, on the other hand, represent what you owe—loans, mortgages, credit card debts. The straightforward formula of Assets minus Liabilities equals your Net Worth is a reflection of your financial health.

Here's a startling fact to ponder: a survey by the Securities and Exchange Board of India (SEBI) found that less than a third of Indians are financially literate and understand these basic concepts. This gap in understanding can lead to decisions that might seem beneficial in the short term but detrimental in the long run. For instance, considering a luxury car as an asset without accounting for its depreciation and the debt incurred to purchase it can skew one's perception of their true financial standing.

The Importance of Emergency Funds

An emergency fund is your financial safety net, designed to cover unexpected expenses like medical emergencies, urgent repairs, or sudden unemployment. The COVID-19 pandemic underscored the unpredictability of life and the critical need for such funds. Experts recommend having at least three to six months' worth of living expenses in an easily accessible savings account.

The Power of Investing Early

Investing early taps into the magic of compound interest, where your investments earn returns, those returns generate their own earnings, and so on. It's why Albert Einstein reportedly called compound interest "the eighth wonder of the world." Starting early gives your investments more time to grow, amplifying the effects of compounding. For instance, investing just ₹5,000 a month at an average return of 8% from age 25 versus starting at age 35 can result in a significant difference by the time you retire.

Exercises to Identify Personal Assets and Liabilities

Exercise 1: Creating Your Financial Balance Sheet

List Your Assets: Start with your most liquid assets (cash, savings accounts) and move towards less liquid assets (stocks, bonds, property).

List Your Liabilities: Begin with short-term liabilities (credit card debt, short-term loans) and list down to long-term liabilities (mortgage, car loans).

Calculate Your Net Worth: Subtract your total liabilities from your total assets.

Exercise 2: Assessing Your Emergency Fund

Calculate Your Monthly Living Expenses: Include everything from rent or mortgage payments to groceries and utility bills.

Evaluate Your Current Emergency Fund: How many months of living expenses can it cover?

Set a Target: If you're below three months, set a plan to reach this initial target. If you're already there, aim for six months.

By understanding and applying these core financial concepts, you're not just managing your money; you're steering your life towards financial freedom and security. It's about making informed decisions today that pave the way for a stable and prosperous tomorrow.

As we emerge from understanding core financial concepts, it's crucial to confront the myths that often cloud our path to financial literacy. These myths, if left unchallenged, can become barriers to our financial growth and well-being.

Myth vs. Reality

Myth: Investing Is Only for the Rich

Reality: The notion that investing is reserved for the wealthy is one of the most pervasive myths. However, the democratization of investing, facilitated by technology, has made it accessible to everyone. Online platforms and apps now allow individuals to start investing with as little as ₹500. A 2019 report by the Association of Mutual Funds in India (AMFI) highlighted a 33% increase in retail investor accounts, showcasing the growing interest among the general public, not just the affluent.

Myth: Saving Money Is Enough for Financial Security

Reality: While saving is an essential part of financial planning, it's not sufficient for long-term financial security on its own. Inflation erodes the value of savings over time, diminishing their purchasing power. Investing, on the other hand, has the potential to outpace inflation and grow your wealth. The World Bank's data reveals that the inflation rate in India averaged around 6.2% from 2010 to 2020, underscoring the need for investments that can offer higher returns.

Exercises to Identify and Transform Limiting Beliefs about Money

Our beliefs about money significantly influence our financial decisions and behaviors. It's time to identify those beliefs that are holding us back and transform them into positive affirmations that empower us.

Exercise 1: Identifying Limiting Beliefs

Write Down Your Beliefs About Money: Spend a few minutes reflecting on what money means to you. Write down statements that come to mind when you think about money, investing, and saving.

Identify the Negative or Limiting Beliefs: Look at your list and highlight any statements that reflect fear, scarcity, or limitations. Common examples include "I'll never be able to afford a house" or "I'm not smart enough to invest."

Exercise 2: Transforming Beliefs into Affirmations

Reframe Each Limiting Belief: For every negative belief, write a positive counter-statement. For instance, "I'll never be able to afford a house" becomes "I am taking steps every day towards saving for my future home."

Create a Habit of Reciting Affirmations: Dedicate a few minutes each day to recite your positive affirmations. This practice can gradually rewire your mindset towards abundance and possibility.

By confronting and debunking these myths, and transforming our limiting beliefs, we unlock the door to a more empowered and financially literate version of ourselves. It's not just about what you earn or save but how you perceive and manage your wealth that defines your financial journey.

Building on the momentum from debunking financial myths and reshaping our limiting beliefs, let's pivot towards a proactive strategy that cements our commitment to financial empowerment. My own journey toward cultivating a growth mindset in wealth maximization was marked by an epiphany: growth and learning in finance are perpetual, driven by curiosity and the relentless pursuit of knowledge.

Actionable Steps to Develop a Growth Mindset

Embarking on this path requires setting tangible, actionable learning goals. Here are strategies that have not only enriched my understanding but have also been transformative for many who embark on this financial literacy voyage.

Commit to Reading One Finance Book a Month

Books are treasure troves of wisdom, offering insights from financial experts and successful investors. They can change the way you think about money, investing, and wealth. For example, "The Richest Man in Babylon" by George S. Clason, offers timeless financial advice through parables set in ancient Babylon, emphasizing the importance of saving, investing, and wise financial planning.

Make it your mission to read at least one finance book a month. Create a list that covers various aspects of personal finance and wealth management. If time is a constraint, audiobooks or book summaries can be incredibly effective alternatives.

Attend Finance Workshops and Webinars

The digital age has democratized access to knowledge, with experts across the globe sharing their insights through workshops and webinars. Participating in these sessions can significantly enhance your understanding of financial concepts and current market trends. Platforms like Coursera and edX offer courses designed by top universities and financial institutions, many of which are free and provide a comprehensive overview of various financial topics.

Adults who receive financial education are more likely to save, invest, and be financially secure. Seek out workshops that offer interactive sessions and Q&A opportunities, allowing you to engage directly with financial experts.

Personalize Your Learning Journey

Reflect on your financial goals and challenges. Tailor your learning to address these areas, whether it's mastering the art of investing, understanding the nuances of tax planning, or becoming more adept at budgeting. The key is to make your learning relevant and aligned with your personal financial aspirations.

Celebrate Your Learning Milestones

Recognize and celebrate each step you take in your financial education journey. Completed a book? Implement a concept you learned from it. These milestones are significant achievements toward developing a robust financial mindset.

Cultivating a growth mindset in finance entails transforming that knowledge into actions that propel you toward your financial goals. It's a journey that I began with simple steps: a book a month, attending workshops, and most importantly, staying curious. These actions are investments in yourself, promising returns that extend far beyond monetary gains. They pave the way to financial independence, resilience, and the realization of your most cherished dreams.

Stories of Transformation: From Financial Confusion to Clarity

Let's dive into expanding our financial smarts together - reading, joining workshops, and really committing to it. But hey, let's not forget to ground all this learning with some real-life transformations. These stories do more than just inspire; they light up the way from being totally baffled about money to having it all figured out. It's all about learning, sticking with it, and making smart plans.

Warren Buffett's journey into finance was fueled by his deep curiosity and a natural knack for numbers. Born in Omaha, Nebraska, Buffett was fascinated by business and investing from a young age. At just six years old, he was already making a profit by selling Coca-Cola bottles. This early experience was just the start of his ventures.

Though his father, Howard Buffett, was a congressman, Warren was more interested in the world of numbers and investment than in politics. Still, his father's stable and supportive background helped Warren nurture his growing passion for finance.

The Turning Point

Buffett's big break wasn't just buying stocks at 11, but his hunger for learning. He started with Cities Service Preferred and then read every book on stocks and wealth in the Omaha public library, some even multiple times. Early on, he realized investing was more about understanding businesses and how the market thinks, not just quick profits.

One pivotal moment in Buffett's early life was his partnership with a high school friend to buy a used pinball machine for $25. They placed it in a local barber shop, and within months, their small venture expanded to several machines across different locations. This experience taught him the value of reinvestment and scaling up operations, lessons that would become hallmarks of his later success.

Actionable Insights

Start Young and Learn from Experience

Buffett's journey underscores the importance of starting financial education as early as possible. It's never too early to learn the basics of saving, investing, and making money work for you. Encouraging young people to take an interest in personal finance, through allowances, savings accounts, and simple investment concepts, can set the foundation for lifelong financial literacy.

Patience and Long-Term Thinking:

Buffett's investment strategy is characterized by patience and a profound understanding of long-term value creation. He famously said, "If you aren't willing to own a stock for ten years, don't even think about owning it for ten minutes." This philosophy of looking beyond the immediate fluctuations and focusing on the intrinsic value of businesses has been central to his success. For individual investors, this underscores the importance of due diligence, research, and a commitment to holding onto investments through market ups and downs.

Buffett's approach to investment, marked by discipline, research, and a focus on long-term value, offers timeless lessons for investors of all ages. By adopting a mindset of learning, patience, and strategic thinking, individuals can navigate the complexities of the financial market and work towards building lasting wealth.

Now, let's explore the financial literacy journeys of an influential figure in the modern finance world: Sallie Krawcheck.

Background

Sallie Krawcheck, once called "The Last Honest Analyst" by Fortune magazine, has held top positions at some of Wall Street's most prestigious firms, including CEO of Merrill Lynch Wealth Management and CFO of Citigroup. Despite her success in the corporate finance world, Krawcheck shifted her focus towards empowering women financially through education and advocacy.

The Turning Point

Krawcheck's pivot came from recognizing the financial industry's gender gap—not just in employment but in financial literacy and investing. She observed that traditional investment platforms often didn't meet women's financial needs or acknowledge their unique challenges. This realization led her to co-found Ellevest in 2016, a digital-first, mission-driven investment platform designed for women. Ellevest emphasizes personalized investment strategies that account for women's longer lifespans, pay gaps, and career breaks.

Actionable Insights

Personalized Financial Planning: Krawcheck's work underscores the importance of personalized financial strategies that consider individual life circumstances. For investors, this means seeking out or creating investment plans that reflect personal goals, risk tolerance, and life stages.

Financial Education as Empowerment: Through Ellevest, Krawcheck has focused on providing financial education specifically tailored to women, addressing topics from investing to negotiating for a raise. Her approach illustrates the power of targeted financial education in empowering individuals to make informed financial decisions.

Advocacy for Inclusivity in Finance: Krawcheck's career transition from Wall Street executive to entrepreneur highlights the importance of advocacy for inclusivity and equality in the financial sector. She demonstrates how leveraging one's platform to address systemic issues can lead to broader societal benefits.

Building on the inspirational journeys of Warren Buffet and Sallie Krawcheck, let's shift our focus inward, to the most critical part of this narrative—your financial journey. Their stories are not just tales of success but are roadmpas, guiding us through the often murky waters of personal finance. Now, it's time to take these lessons and forge our path, using their insights to illuminate our way.

Reflecting on Your Financial Situation

Just like Sallie and Warren made their mark in the finance world, you've got what it takes to shape your own financial future. So, what's the first step? Taking a good, hard look at where you're at and where you want to be.

Exercise 1: Financial Self-Assessment

Identify Your Financial Goals: What are you aiming for? Retirement savings, education for your children, a home, travel? List these goals in order of priority.

Assess Your Current Financial Health: Using a simple spreadsheet or a personal finance app, track your assets (what you own) and liabilities (what you owe). This snapshot will give you a clearer picture of your net worth.

Evaluate Your Income vs. Expenses: Are you living within your means, or are you skating on the thin ice of debt? This exercise is about honesty and recognition, setting the stage for actionable change.

Exercise 2: Learning from Leaders

Emulate Financially Empowering Habits: Inspired by Krawcheck, start with educating yourself on investment options tailored to your unique situation. Begin with small, consistent investments to harness the power of compound interest.

Diversify Your Learning: Just as you would diversify an investment portfolio, diversify your financial education sources. Attend workshops, read books, listen to podcasts—immerse yourself in the world of finance.

Mindset Shift: As we have previously reinforced, identify any fear-based beliefs holding you back and replace them with empowering affirmations.

Now, with these exercises and reflections, you're an active participant in your financial narrative. By applying these tools to your life, you're charting your course, informed by their wisdom but tailored to your dreams. Your financial journey is uniquely yours, rich with potential and ripe for growth. Let's step forward with confidence, armed with knowledge, inspired by success, and driven by a clear vision of our financial future.

Chapter 2

Your Money Blueprint

Imagine charting a road trip tailored just for you, where the journey to your financial future isn't just about reaching a destination but about making stops that spark joy and resonate with your deepest passions. This adventure isn't a race; it's about forging a path that mirrors your life's values and fills you with satisfaction. Let's explore how to shape your unique vision for financial success, focusing on practical steps and insights to make the journey both thorough and intimately yours.

Personalising Your Financial Vision

Why a Personal Vision Matters

Your financial vision is more than numbers on a page; it's the embodiment of your aspirations and what you cherish most. It's about envisioning a future where financial worries don't dictate your choices—a future where you're free to pursue your passions, support your loved ones, and contribute to causes you believe in. This vision guides your financial decisions and strategies.

Step-by-Step Guide to Crafting Your Vision

- **Reflect on What Truly Matters:** Take a moment to think about what gives you joy and purpose. Is it the freedom to travel, the ability to write and create, or the security to provide for your family's needs without stress? These reflections are the bedrock of your financial vision.

- **Visualize Your Ideal Future:** Envision your life in the next 5 to 20 years, but ground this vision in realism. Imagine a typical day in this ideal future: Where are you? Who are you with? What are you doing? How does financial stability enable this lifestyle?

- **Draft Your Vision Statement:** Based on your reflections and visualization, draft a statement that captures your ideal financial future. Make it specific and evocative, something that stirs you to action. For instance, "I envision a future where I'm free to explore the world, create without financial constraints, and provide a nurturing and enriching environment for my family."

Setting SMART Financial Goals

To turn your vision into reality, you'll need to set concrete, actionable goals. The SMART framework isn't just a tool; it's your roadmap for breaking down your vision into achievable milestones.

- **Specific:** Define what success looks like. For example, "Save ₹50,000 for a down payment on a home in the next two years."

- **Measurable:** Attach numbers to your goals to track progress. "Increase my emergency fund to cover six months' living expenses."

- **Achievable:** Ensure your goals are realistic, considering your current financial situation and commitments.

- **Relevant:** Align every goal with your broader vision. Each goal should be a stepping stone towards your ideal future.

- **Time-bound:** Set deadlines. "Save ₹50,000 for my downpayment within the next 9 months."

Templates and Prompts

To help articulate your goals, use templates or journals designed for financial planning. Begin with broad questions that connect with your inner motivations, then narrow down to specifics. Prompts like "How does my ideal day in my future look, and what role does financial stability play in it?" can offer insights into shaping your goals.

By adopting a structured yet deeply personal approach to defining your financial vision and goals, you're crafting a future that resonates with who you are and what you value most. This clarity motivates you and simplifies complex financial decisions, making the journey towards your goals a meaningful and fulfilling adventure.

Let's take a moment and reflect on the journey we've begun together, steering towards crafting a personal vision for financial success. As we chart this course, there's a crucial aspect we need to address—the psychology of our spending and saving habits. Picture this: just as a ship needs to be mindful of the undercurrents to avoid being led astray, we must be aware of the psychological forces shaping our financial decisions.

I've noticed in my own journey, and perhaps you have too, how a fleeting emotion can lead to an unplanned purchase, transforming a moment of joy into a lingering worry. It's a common story, and not just among a few of us. A LendingTree survey revealed that 69% of Americans admit their emotions have swayed their spending habits, with 76% of emotional spenders acknowledging that it often leads to overspending. This isn't a phenomenon confined to the shores of the United States; it's a global tide, affecting individuals in both developed and developing countries, including India.

In today's world, where the ease of one-click online shopping and mobile wallets tempts us at every turn, managing our finances requires more than just discipline; it demands mindfulness. This approach, typically reserved for our eating and self-care routines, can be a crucial anchor for our financial health.

Understanding Emotional Intelligence

At the heart of this mindfulness is emotional intelligence—the compass that helps us navigate the sea of our emotions. Emotional intelligence isn't just about controlling our impulses; it's about understanding why we feel compelled to spend in the first place. It's recognizing that moment of emotional spending before it translates into an action.

Research underscores the power of emotional intelligence in curbing our materialistic and compulsive buying tendencies. Those who can manage their emotions well tend to exhibit lower levels of materialism and are less prone to impulsive buying. It's about achieving a state of financial consciousness, where every decision is made from a place of clarity and rationality, rather than fleeting desires.

Strategies to Manage Emotional Spending

Identify Emotional Triggers: Start by recognizing the emotions that lead you to spend. Is it stress, happiness, sadness, or perhaps boredom? Understanding these triggers is the first step in managing them.

Pause Before You Purchase: Implement a mandatory waiting period for all non-essential purchases. Even a brief pause can help you assess whether the spending aligns with your financial goals and values.

Reflect on Your Spending: Keep a journal of your purchases and how they made you feel. Over time, you'll begin to see patterns, helping you to identify and address the underlying emotions.

Set Spending Rules: Establish clear guidelines for your spending. This could be a weekly or monthly budget for discretionary expenses, or rules like 'only buy it if you've thought about it for more than 24 hours'.

Seek Alternatives for Emotional Relief: Find other ways to cope with your emotions, such as talking to a friend, going for a walk, or practicing meditation. These can offer the solace you might seek from shopping.

Practice Gratitude: Regularly reflecting on what you're thankful for can shift your focus from what you want to what you already have, reducing the urge to make unnecessary purchases.

Adopting these strategies enriches our journey towards financial success with deeper self-awareness and satisfaction. As we move forward, let's embrace the principles of emotional intelligence, nas a tool for financial stability and as a cornerstone for a life led by intention and fulfillment.

Let's take a step back and refocus on the essence of building a solid financial foundation: the formation of habits. Just as in any aspect of life, the habits we cultivate around our finances—how we save, spend, and manage money—are pivotal to achieving our broader financial vision. Integrating insights from the field of psychology and leveraging modern tools can significantly enhance our ability to form and sustain these crucial habits.

Understanding Habit Formation in Finance

Financial habits, whether it's saving a portion of your paycheck or curbing impulse purchases, are formed through repeated behavior in response to specific cues and are reinforced by the rewards they bring. Recognizing and adjusting these cues and rewards can transform our financial health, leading to better money management and growth over time.

Automating Savings

While tools like Chime, Digit, and Acorns offer a hands-off approach to saving, they're not universally effective. A study by Case Western Reserve University illuminates this point, suggesting that while these tools can facilitate saving for some, they act merely as a stopgap for others. The convenience of automated saving, facilitated by the ubiquity of online banking and smartphone apps, is undeniable. Yet, it's essential to remember that these tools serve best when complemented by a conscious effort to save.

The Habit of Regular Saving

Saving money consistently is similar to laying bricks for the foundation of your financial house. It's essential for both weathering storms and building towards future dreams. If automatic saving tools don't quite work for you, consider manually setting up a recurring transfer to your savings account each payday. This "pay yourself first" approach ensures that saving becomes as routine as paying your bills.

Mindful Spending Through Budgeting Apps

In managing finances, awareness is key. Budgeting apps serve as our modern-day ledger, providing a clear view of our financial landscape. These apps not only categorize expenses automatically but also allow for a deep dive into where our money goes each month. By making budgeting a daily practice, we cultivate a habit of mindful spending, steering clear of financial pitfalls and aligning our expenditures with our values and goals.

Minimizing High-Interest Debt

Debt management is crucial in our financial habit toolkit. High-interest debts, like those from credit cards, can quickly become overwhelming due to compounding interest. Understanding the terms of your debts and prioritizing repayments can save you from financial strain. Strategies like paying more than the minimum payment or considering debt consolidation can provide a clearer path out of debt.

Daily Financial Vigilance

Just as we might routinely check our email or social media, making a habit of checking our bank accounts daily can lead to better financial health. This practice helps us catch unauthorized transactions early and stay aware of our spending patterns, reducing the risk of overdraft fees and keeping us on track with our financial goals.

The 24-Hour Rule

Impulse spending is often a reaction to emotional cues rather than rational decisions. By applying the 24-hour rule to potential purchases, we give ourselves time to consider if an item is truly needed or if it's merely a fleeting desire. This pause can significantly reduce unnecessary spending, aligning our habits more closely with our financial vision.

In my own journey, these strategies have transformed both my bank balance and my relationship with money. Automating savings freed me from the worry of whether I was saving enough each month. Budgeting apps turned the once overwhelming task of tracking expenses into an insightful daily ritual. And the 24-hour rule? It's saved me more times than I can count from purchases that would have brought momentary joy but long-term regret.

Adopting these habits doesn't happen overnight, but with persistence and the right tools, anyone can rewire their financial habits for the better. As we continue on this journey, remember that each small step towards better money management is a leap towards realizing your financial vision and achieving true financial freedom.

Designing a Budget That Grows with You

As we pivot from the broader strokes of setting financial goals and finding our way through the psychological terrain of spending and saving, we find ourselves at the doorstep of an essential financial practice: budgeting. Creating a budget that fits your current lifestyle and adapts with you over time is crucial for financial planning. The budgeting methods we'll discuss are designed to help you through both stable and challenging financial situations.

The 50/30/20 Rule: A Balanced Approach

Diving deeper into the 50/30/20 rule, let's explore how this balanced approach to budgeting can be applied in a real-world context, making it more tangible and relatable for you.

50% on Needs: Allocating half of your income to necessities ensures that your fundamental needs are always met without compromising. For instance, if your monthly take-home pay is ₹50,000, you'd allocate ₹25,000 to cover rent or mortgage, groceries, utility bills, and transportation costs. It's about securing your basics first—ensuring that no matter what, you and your family have a roof over your heads, food on the table, and the means to get to work or school.

30% on Wants: This is where budgeting becomes more personalized and, dare I say, fun. With ₹15,000 from the same paycheck, you have the freedom to explore what brings you happiness outside of your basic needs. Whether it's subscribing to streaming services, dining at your favorite restaurants, or pursuing a hobby like photography or gardening, this portion of your budget celebrates the joys that make life rich and fulfilling. It's about balancing the discipline of budgeting with the freedom to enjoy the fruits of your labor.

20% on Savings and Debt Repayment: The remaining ₹10,000 is your future fund—money you set aside for savings, investments, and paying off any debts faster than the minimum payments. This could mean contributing to your retirement fund, building an emergency savings account, or tackling high-interest credit card debt. It's about creating a buffer that protects you from unforeseen financial shocks and investing in your future self.

Making the 50/30/20 Rule Work for You

Adopting the 50/30/20 rule isn't about rigid adherence to percentages but about finding a balance that suits your individual circumstances. Here are some ways to tailor the rule to fit your life:

Adjust the Percentages as Needed: Life isn't static, and neither should your budget be. If you live in a city with high living costs, you might need to adjust the percentages to allocate more to your needs. Conversely, if you're focusing on debt repayment, you might choose to increase the percentage of income directed toward debts and savings.

Use Budgeting Tools: Numerous apps and online tools can help you apply the 50/30/20 rule effectively. By linking your bank accounts and tracking your spending, these tools can automatically categorize your expenditures and provide insights into how well you're adhering to your budgeting goals.

Regular Reviews: Your financial situation will evolve—raises, job changes, or new family responsibilities will affect your budget. Regularly reviewing and adjusting your budget ensures that the 50/30/20 rule continues to work for you, helping you meet your financial goals and adapting to life's changes.

In my experience, the beauty of the 50/30/20 rule lies in its simplicity and flexibility. It has allowed me to demystify the budgeting process, creating a clear structure for managing my finances while still enjoying the present and planning for the future. It's a reminder that effective budgeting isn't about restriction; it's about making informed choices that align with both your immediate happiness and long-term well-being.

Zero-Based Budgeting

Zero-based budgeting is like giving every rupee you earn a specific mission before the month even begins. It's a strategy that doesn't allow for loose ends or vague categories. Instead, every rupee is tasked with a job, be it covering a bill, contributing to savings, or paying down debt. This meticulous approach ensures that by the end of the month, the equation of income minus expenditures equals zero—every rupee is accounted for. Let's dive into how to implement this method and make it work for you.

Listing Monthly Income: Start with a comprehensive tally of your income. This isn't just about the paycheck from your 9-to-5. Include any side hustles, freelance work, and passive income streams like dividends from investments or rental income. For instance, if you're a graphic designer by day and a tutor on weekends, both income sources form the foundation of your budgeting plan.

Detailing Every Expense: This step goes beyond just noting down your rent and utility bills. You need to consider every possible expenditure, including those that don't come up monthly. Annual subscriptions for software you use, quarterly insurance payments, or even the yearly renewal fee for your credit card—these are all part of the picture. By accounting for these irregular expenses, you're less likely to be caught off guard.

Assigning Every Rupee a Role: With your income and expenses laid out, the next step is to assign every rupee a specific role. This is where zero-based budgeting really shines. It forces you to think critically about how you're using your money. Allocating funds to your needs, wants, savings, and debt repayments requires intentionality. If there's leftover money, it doesn't just sit idly in your account; you find it a purpose. Maybe it boosts your emergency fund, or perhaps it accelerates your debt repayment plan.

Adopting zero-based budgeting doesn't just magically solve all financial challenges. It requires discipline and a bit of effort, especially in the initial stages as you're mapping out your income and expenses. However, this level of detail provides clarity and control over your finances that few other methods can match.

Customization Is Key: One of the strengths of zero-based budgeting is its adaptability. Depending on your financial goals and circumstances, you can tweak your budget. If saving for a down payment on a house is a priority, you might allocate a larger portion of your income to savings after covering your essential expenses.

Tools to Ease the Process: Leveraging budgeting apps and software can simplify the process of implementing a zero-based budget. Many apps categorize expenses automatically and can help you keep track of irregular spending patterns, making it easier to adjust your budget in real-time.

In my journey with zero-based budgeting, the initial setup was indeed time-consuming. However, the insight it provided into my spending habits was invaluable. I discovered subscriptions

I had forgotten about and expenses that didn't align with my current priorities. Allocating every rupee a role helped me take control of my finances in a way I hadn't before—it was like having a detailed map for my financial journey.

Zero-based budgeting is indeed a mindset that encourages active engagement with your finances. By ensuring every rupee has a job, you'remaking the most of your current income and paving the way for a secure financial future. Whether you're saving for a dream vacation, planning for retirement, or working towards being debt-free, zero-based budgeting can be a powerful ally on your financial journey.

The Envelope System: Tangible Money Management

For those who prefer a more tactile approach, the envelope system brings budgeting to life. This method involves dividing your cash into envelopes, each labeled for a specific spending category (e.g., groceries, entertainment). Once an envelope is empty, that's your cue to stop spending in that category for the month. It's particularly effective for managing variable expenses and curbing overspending.

Diving into the world of budgeting can often feel like finding your way through a maze without a map, especially if you're charting this territory for the first time or adjusting to significant life changes. The Consumer Financial Protection Bureau (CFPB) underscores the essence of budgeting beautifully—it's about creating a balance that covers your needs, fulfills your wants, and still allows you to tuck away savings for what lies ahead.

Step-by-Step Approach to Implementing Your Budgeting Strategy

Calculating Your Monthly Income: The first step in crafting any budget that works for you is getting a clear picture of your total monthly income. This includes the salary from your day job and any side hustles, passive income like rental earnings, dividends from investments, or even occasional freelancing gigs. For example, if you're a software developer who also tutors on weekends and invests in the stock market, all these sources contribute to your financial canvas.

Identifying and Categorizing Expenses: Once you know what you're working with income-wise, the next step is to map out where that money goes. Breaking down your spending into categories—housing, utilities, groceries, transportation, entertainment, and so on—helps in pinpointing areas where you might be overspending or underspending. It's not uncommon to discover that what you thought was a minor monthly subscription is actually chipping away a significant chunk of your budget.

Adjusting as Needed: Life is anything but static, and your budget should reflect that dynamism. An unexpected job change, a new family member, or even a sudden interest in a costly hobby—these life events necessitate a revisit to your budget. The key here is flexibility; your budget is a living document that should evolve as your life does.

Keeping Track

Monitoring Your Spending: With the blueprint of your budget in place, the ongoing task is to ensure you're sticking to it. This is where technology can be a great ally. Budgeting apps and digital tools offer a seamless way to keep tabs on your expenses, categorizing them automatically and even setting alerts for when you're nearing your spending limits in various categories. For those who find solace in the tangible, maintaining a handwritten ledger or notebook serves the same purpose, fostering a closer, more personal connection with your spending habits.

Choosing a System That Resonates: The effectiveness of a budgeting tool is in how well it aligns with your lifestyle and preferences. Whether you opt for the sophistication of a digital app or the simplicity of a notebook, the crux is consistency. Regularly updating and reviewing your budget is what transforms it from a mere document into a powerful financial tool.

In my own journey, transitioning from an ad-hoc approach to a structured budgeting strategy was a revelation. It was like turning on a flashlight in a dim room; suddenly, I could see clearly where my money was going, and more importantly, why. This clarity didn't just help in managing my finances better; it empowered me to make decisions that were aligned with my long-term goals and dreams.

Leveraging Technology for Smarter Budgeting

In the age where almost every aspect of our lives is complemented by an app, it's no surprise that managing our finances has also taken a digital turn. The right budgeting app can be like having a financial advisor in your pocket, guiding you, nudging you towards healthier spending habits, and illuminating the path to achieving your financial goals. Let's explore some tools that could be your allies in this journey of financial mindfulness.

Money View: Expense Manager App

Imagine a dashboard that categorizes your expenses from food orders to mobile recharges and nudges you towards smarter investment choices. Money View does just that. It's like having a bird's-eye view of your financial landscape, where you can track your spending in real-time and even explore investment avenues like mutual funds. For those looking to consolidate debts or finance big purchases, Money View also offers loan options.

Goodbudget: Budget & Finance App

Drawing inspiration from the traditional envelope budgeting system, Goodbudget digitizes this approach, allowing you to allocate funds across different spending categories. It's particularly handy for families or roommates, as it syncs across multiple devices, enabling everyone involved to stay on the same financial page. Think of it as your digital envelope system, fostering a collaborative approach to budgeting and spending.

Wallet: Budget Expense Tracker

Wallet transforms the complex world of personal finance into an intuitive, easy-to-navigate experience. By syncing with your bank, it automates the tracking of your spending and provides insights that help you adapt your budget flexibly. Planning payments and diving into insightful reports becomes a breeze. Sharing certain features with loved ones, it also becomes a tool for managing collective budgets, reinforcing the adage that teamwork makes the dream work.

Spending Tracker

For those who prefer simplicity, Spending Tracker is a godsend. It's designed to effortlessly manage your spending across different time frames – daily, weekly, monthly, or even yearly. Its straightforward interface allows for quick logging of expenses and income, making it ideal for someone just embarking on their budgeting journey. The Pro Upgrade elevates this experience by enabling syncing across devices, ensuring your budgeting efforts are seamlessly integrated into your lifestyle.

Monefy: Money Manager

Monefy demystifies the budgeting process with its simple interface and easy expense entry. It's like having a financial journal where every entry offers clarity on your spending habits. Supporting multiple accounts, Monefy provides a visual feast through detailed charts, helping you see at a glance where your money flows each month.

Fudget

Fudget's charm lies in its simplicity and effectiveness. It strips down budgeting to its core, making it accessible for everyone. Whether you're setting up recurring payments or need a quick summary of your expenses, Fudget delivers. Its free version offers a robust set of features, while the premium version adds layers of functionality for those seeking more depth in their budgeting tools.

TrackWallet: Expense Tracker & More

For the meticulous planner, TrackWallet offers a comprehensive platform to monitor income, plan expenditures, and track budgets in real-time. It stands out by offering detailed reports that not only cover profits and losses but also provide insights into budgeting efficiency. It's like having a financial analyst at your fingertips, ready to decode the numbers and guide your spending decisions.

Expenses Manager: Fast & Easy

Designed for the fast-paced individual, Expenses Manager simplifies tracking your monthly cash flow. Its ability to provide weekly and monthly reports makes it easier to spot trends in your spending and savings, acting as a catalyst for informed financial decisions.

Dreamfora: AI Goal Setting

In a league of its own, Dreamfora takes goal setting to the next level with AI. It's about aligning your financial habits with your dreams. By breaking down your financial goals into actionable steps, Dreamfora adds a layer of motivation and structure to your financial planning efforts.

Choosing the right app from this plethora of options depends on your personal finance goals, habits, and preferences. Whether you need a simple spending tracker or a comprehensive budgeting solution, there's an app designed to meet your needs. As we integrate these tools into our daily routines, we unlock the potential to manage our finances more effectively and to craft a life that aligns with our deepest aspirations.

Reward Systems for Budgeting Success

Your journey of financial discipline and budgeting requires patience, perseverance, and, most importantly, a series of lighthouses along the way—reward systems that illuminate the path and keep us anchored in our commitment. Just as small harbors provide respite and celebration for sailors, setting up reward systems for budgeting milestones can inject joy and motivation into what might otherwise feel like a daunting task.

The principle behind reward systems is deeply rooted in behavioral psychology. Positive reinforcement, the process of encouraging a certain behavior through rewards, plays a pivotal role. When we reward ourselves for staying under budget or hitting a savings goal, we're reinforcing the behavior that got us there.

Crafting Effective Reward Systems for Budgeting

Setting Specific Milestones

Effective reward systems start with setting clear, quantifiable milestones in your budgeting journey. For instance, if your goal is to reduce dining out expenses, a specific milestone could be cutting this spending by 20% over the next month. It's essential that these milestones are achievable and measurable, providing a clear target to aim for.

Choosing Meaningful Rewards

The power of a reward lies in its ability to motivate you towards your goal. If you've successfully met your target of reducing dining out expenses, consider a reward that feels indulgent but doesn't counteract your progress. Perhaps, if you've saved ₹2000 in a month by dining out less, allocate ₹500 of that saved money to purchase a gourmet ingredient to cook a special meal at home. This type of reward reinforces your success without undermining the financial habits you're working to build.

Maintaining Balance in Rewards

The scale of the reward should match the achievement. Minor milestones might be celebrated with small, simple pleasures, such as an evening spent at your favorite local park or an at-home spa night. For more significant achievements, like reaching a six-month continuous saving streak, the reward could be more substantial, yet still within reason—perhaps a one-day local getaway.

Incorporating Non-Monetary Rewards

Not all rewards need to involve spending money. Completing a month of meticulous budget tracking could be celebrated with a 'me day,' dedicated to your hobbies or relaxation. This approach not only conserves financial resources but also emphasizes the intrinsic value of personal time and well-being.

Incorporating a reward system into your budgeting routine transforms the process from a mere financial task to an engaging and rewarding challenge. For example, when I set a goal to increase my savings rate by 5% over three months, I promised myself a new book by my favorite author if successful. Each time I opted not to make an impulsive purchase, I visualized the enjoyment of achieving my goal and the reward awaiting me. This personal commitment turned budgeting into a game where the prize was not just the book, but the satisfaction of knowing I was making tangible progress towards my financial independence.

Reward systems work because they tap into the brain's reward pathways. Achieving a budgeting milestone and receiving a reward releases dopamine, a neurotransmitter associated with feelings of pleasure and satisfaction. This positive reinforcement makes the act of budgeting and meeting financial goals more desirable, encouraging the repetition of these behaviors.

As we go through the rewarding journey of budgeting, celebrating milestones and leveraging tools to stay on track, it's pivotal to recognize that life is in constant flux. Amidst this financial journey of ours, there lies a crucial aspect that demands our attention: adjusting our budget to accommodate significant life events such as marriage, career changes, and the addition of children. These events are transformative experiences that necessitate a reevaluation of our financial strategies.

The Importance of Regular Budget Reviews

Life's significant events underscore the necessity of treating your budget as a living document. Regularly revisiting and revising your budget allows you to stay aligned with your evolving financial goals and realities. Just as we routinely check our vehicles or gadgets for necessary updates and maintenance, our budgets too require periodic reviews to ensure they remain relevant and effective.

How Often Should You Review? While there's no one-size-fits-all answer, a good rule of thumb is to review your budget at least quarterly. However, during periods of rapid change or ahead of major life events, more frequent reviews may be warranted.

Embracing Flexibility: Adjusting your budget isn't about scrapping your goals but about adapting your strategies to meet your goals despite life's changes. Flexibility is key. As your priorities shift, so too will the allocation of your resources.

This adaptability is not a sign of failure but of smart financial management.

Reflecting on my own life's journey, each significant event—be it career milestones or personal ones like marriage—served as a prompt to revisit my budget. These were vital opportunities to ensure my financial plan remained in harmony with my life's evolving narrative.

Life will always be full of surprises and shifts, but with a budget that's regularly revisited and revised, you're better equipped to navigate these changes without losing sight of your financial goals.

Managing your finances through life's ups and downs is challenging. It's essential to adjust your budget for major life events and manage the stress that comes with financial uncertainty. Financial stress can impair your judgment, complicating decision-making. However, employing effective strategies can help you manage your finances with calmness and clarity.

Techniques for Managing Financial Stress

Stress Budgeting: This involves creating a budget specifically designed to reduce financial stress. It's about prioritizing expenses that directly contribute to your well-being and mental health, such as a modest budget for activities that help you relax or hobbies that bring you joy. The goal is to ensure that, despite financial constraints, there's room in your budget for self-care.

Consulting a Financial Advisor: Sometimes, the best way to tackle financial stress is to seek guidance from professionals. A financial advisor can offer a fresh perspective on your financial situation, helping you to see options you might have missed. They can also assist in creating a realistic plan to meet your financial goals, providing clarity and reducing stress.

Leveraging Financial Wellness Apps: Many apps today are designed for promoting financial wellness. These apps often include features like personalized financial tips, stress management techniques, and even access to financial advisors. Incorporating these tools into your financial strategy can provide ongoing support and insights, making the journey less daunting.

In moments of financial stress, I've found solace in setting aside time each week to review my finances calmly. This ritual, coupled with the use of a financial wellness app, transformed my approach from reactive to proactive. The app's reminders to review my expenses and its tips for managing stress were like having a financial coach by my side, guiding me through turbulent times.

Remember, managing financial stress is not about ignoring the storms but about learning to sail in spite of them. The techniques outlined above are tools in your arsenal, helping you maintain your course towards financial well-being.

As we wrap up our discussion, let me leave you with a reminder that true financial peace comes from living within our means, investing in our future, and finding joy in the journey. In the words of Dave Ramsey, "Financial peace isn't the acquisition of stuff. It's learning to live on less than you make, so you can give money back and have money to invest. You can't win until you do this."

Chapter 3

Wealth Wisdom: Lessons from the Past and Present

Finding your way through the domain of investments can often feel like deciphering an ancient code, where understanding the potential growth of your assets is crucial. Among the various tools at an investor's disposal, the Rule of 72 stands out for its simplicity and effectiveness in shedding light on the future of our investments. This rule offers a straightforward method to gauge how long it will take for an investment to double in value, providing a snapshot of potential growth that's easy to comprehend.

The Essence of the Rule of 72

The Rule of 72 is a remarkably simple mathematical formula designed to estimate the number of years required to double the invested money at a fixed annual rate of interest. By dividing 72 by the annual rate of return, investors can get a rough estimate of how many years it will take for their initial investment to grow twofold.

Let's dive into how this rule works in practice. Suppose you have an investment that yields an 8% annual rate of return. By dividing 72 by 8, you arrive at 9. This result indicates that it will take approximately 9 years for your investment to double in value.

This rule applies to positive growth and can also be used to understand the impact of inflation on savings. For instance, if the inflation rate is 4%, using the Rule of 72, you can determine that the purchasing power of your money would halve in about 18 years.

The Power of Compound Interest

The underlying principle that makes the Rule of 72 so valuable is the concept of compound interest. Compound interest, often hailed as the eighth wonder of the world, signifies the process where the interest earned on an investment is reinvested to generate additional interest over time. This concept is crucial for understanding how investments grow exponentially, rather than linearly, over periods.

For example, a small, consistent investment in a mutual fund or retirement account that yields an average of 6% annual interest will double in roughly 12 years according to the Rule of 72. If you continue to let it grow, without adding any additional funds, it would quadruple from the initial investment in about 24 years.

Considerations and Limitations

While the Rule of 72 provides a quick and easy way to estimate investment growth, it's essential to remember that it offers an approximation, not a precise prediction. The actual time it takes for an investment to double can vary based on numerous factors including market volatility, interest rates changes, and capital gains tax, among others.

Moreover, the rule becomes less accurate at very high rates of return. Therefore, while it's a valuable tool for quick calculations and comparisons, it should be used alongside other financial planning and analysis methods for a comprehensive understanding of investment growth.

The Rule of 72 demystifies the complex world of investments, offering a lens through which individuals can envision the potential growth of their assets. Understanding this rule is a stepping stone to making informed, strategic investment choices that align with one's financial goals and timelines. It reinforces the importance of patience and long-term planning in the journey to financial prosperity, reminding us that the most significant rewards often come to those who wait.

In the continuum of investment growth, where the Rule of 72 provides a glimpse into the future potential of our assets, understanding the intricate balance between risk and reward is paramount. This balance is the linchpin in the machinery of financial planning, ensuring that the pursuit of returns does not leave us vulnerable to unforeseen pitfalls.

The Risk vs. Reward Spectrum

The relationship between risk and reward in investing is fundamental yet complex. Generally, higher potential returns come with higher risks. This means that investments with the capability to double your money quicker inherently carry a greater chance of significant losses. Conversely, lower-risk investments typically offer more modest returns but with increased stability.

To navigate this spectrum effectively, one must first assess their risk tolerance. This assessment involves understanding your financial goals, investment timeline, and emotional capacity to withstand market fluctuations. A young investor saving for retirement may have a higher risk tolerance and opt for aggressive growth stocks, while someone nearing retirement might prioritize capital preservation, leaning towards bonds or fixed deposits.

The Role of an Emergency Fund

In balancing risk and reward, the creation and maintenance of an emergency fund cannot be overstated. An emergency fund acts as a financial buffer, safeguarding you from having to dip into investments during times of need, which could be during market downturns when withdrawal would mean locking in losses.

Financial experts recommend setting aside enough cash to cover 3 to 6 months' worth of living expenses. This fund should be easily accessible, kept in a savings account or a money market fund that offers stability and liquidity. The presence of this fund ensures that you can navigate life's unexpected turns without jeopardizing your long-term investment strategy.

Incorporating Risk Management Strategies

Once you have established an emergency fund, employing risk management strategies within your investment portfolio is crucial. Diversification is a key tactic; spreading your investments across various asset classes can reduce the impact of poor performance in any single investment on your overall portfolio.

Another strategy is asset allocation, which involves adjusting the mix of assets like stocks, bonds, and cash in your portfolio based on your risk tolerance, investment goals, and timeline.

This allocation should be revisited regularly, as shifts in the market and changes in your personal circumstances may necessitate adjustments.

The journey towards financial prosperity is marked by the dual forces of risk and reward. Understanding and managing this dynamic is crucial in developing a robust investment strategy. By assessing personal risk tolerance, creating a safety net through an emergency fund, and employing strategies like diversification and asset allocation, investors can strive for optimal returns while safeguarding against undue risk. Remember, in the realm of investing, risk is a constant companion to reward, and finding your balance between the two is key to achieving long-term financial success.

The foundation of traditional investment strategies often involves a mix of stocks, bonds, cash equivalents, and real estate. However, as the financial world evolves, it's essential to incorporate modern asset classes like cryptocurrencies and tech stocks to stay aligned with current opportunities and challenges.

Adapting Traditional Investment Strategies

Diversification with Modern Asset Classes

A key principle of investing is diversification, aimed at spreading risks across various asset classes to achieve a balanced risk-return portfolio profile. Incorporating modern assets like cryptocurrencies and tech stocks can enhance this diversification.

Cryptocurrencies: Assets like Bitcoin and Ethereum add a new dimension to diversification. Their performance tends to have a low correlation with traditional assets, making them useful for spreading risk. However, their notable volatility suggests a cautious approach, typically recommending a small allocation within a portfolio.

Tech Stocks: The technology sector, including companies listed on NASDAQ, has shown strong growth potential. While these stocks may experience more significant fluctuations compared to the broader market, they offer the potential for substantial long-term gains. Including tech stocks within the equity portion of a portfolio focuses on growth but necessitates awareness of their volatility.

Asset Allocation Adjustments

Integrating modern asset classes into your investment strategy requires reevaluating your asset allocation to ensure it aligns with your risk tolerance and investment goals.

Risk Tolerance: The addition of volatile assets like cryptocurrencies should reflect your comfort with risk. A conservative investor might allocate a smaller percentage to these assets, whereas a more aggressive investor could afford a larger allocation.

Time Horizon: Your investment timeline also influences how you incorporate modern asset classes. Investors with a longer horizon may be more equipped to handle the short-term volatility of tech stocks and cryptocurrencies, anticipating upward trends over time.

Leveraging Technology for Investment

Modern investment strategies often use technology for research, trading, and managing portfolios. Robo-advisors, for instance, can automatically include modern asset classes in portfolios based on factors like risk tolerance and investment objectives.

Continuous Education and Research

Staying informed about developments in cryptocurrencies and the tech sector is crucial. This means understanding the basics of blockchain technology and keeping abreast of trends in the tech industry, which can influence investment decisions.

Regulatory and Tax Considerations

Being aware of the regulatory environment for cryptocurrencies and tech investments is vital, as this can significantly impact your strategy. The legal status of cryptocurrencies varies globally, and specific tax implications exist for trading and holding these assets.

Examples of Adapted Investment Strategies

A balanced portfolio might keep a traditional stocks-to-bonds ratio but include a 5% allocation to cryptocurrencies, adding potential for higher returns while managing overall risk.

An investor focusing on growth might overweight their portfolio in tech stocks, especially those showing strong fundamentals and growth prospects, while still maintaining a balance with more stable assets.

Incorporating modern asset classes like cryptocurrencies and tech stocks into traditional investment strategies involves thoughtful consideration of diversification, asset allocation, and risk management. By carefully integrating these assets, investors can potentially enhance returns and navigate the complexities of today's investment landscape. However, it's critical to stay informed about these assets' unique characteristics and risks and to seek advice from financial professionals as needed.

The landscape of real estate investment in India has undergone substantial transformation, especially with the advent of Real Estate Investment Trusts (REITs) and crowdfunding platforms. These innovations have revolutionized how individuals can participate in real estate markets, offering new paths to investment that are more accessible and diversified.

Evolution of Real Estate Investment Strategies

Post-Independence Era: Initially, the focus in India's real estate sector was on developing new state capitals and supporting industrialization. This period saw the expansion of cities and a growing demand for commercial and residential spaces. The government played a significant role in shaping the industry through policy and the establishment of sector-specific institutions.

Economic Liberalization and REITs: The liberalization of the 1990s marked a pivotal shift, welcoming multinational corporations and foreign investment and spurring commercial real estate development. The introduction of REITs provided a structured and regulated investment avenue, allowing individuals to invest in real estate markets previously accessible only to those with significant capital.

Modern-Day REITs in India

REITs have become a cornerstone of modern real estate investment in India. With SEBI's guidelines established in 2015 and revised in 2019 to lower the minimum investment required, REITs have become more accessible to the average investor. These trusts offer the opportunity to invest in premier real estate, with the benefits of earning dividend income and potential capital appreciation. Moreover, they're mandated to distribute at least 90% of their income to investors, making them an attractive option for income-seeking individuals.

Crowdfunding Platforms

Crowdfunding platforms have further democratized real estate investment, enabling individuals with smaller amounts of capital to gain exposure to the real estate sector. These platforms connect investors with developers, allowing for fractional ownership of property investments. This method of investing offers the advantages of transparency, ease of investment, and risk diversification across multiple projects.

Application of Modern Real Estate Investment Strategies

Diversification through REITs: Including REITs in an investment portfolio allows for diversification across various real estate assets, such as commercial spaces and residential complexes. This strategy helps in spreading risk and reducing exposure to any single investment.

Accessibility and Liquidity: REITs are listed on stock exchanges, which enhances liquidity and allows investors to buy or sell units with ease, contrasting with the traditionally illiquid nature of direct real estate investments.

Crowdfunding Advantages: Real estate crowdfunding offers several benefits, including the ability to invest in multiple projects, ease of entry and exit through platforms offering secondary market trading, and risk distribution among a larger pool of investors.

Regulatory Framework and Taxation

The regulatory and tax environment in India has evolved to support these new investment avenues. Reforms such as the GST and digitization of financial transactions have streamlined processes, making it easier for investors to participate in the real estate market. While REITs present certain tax advantages, investors should also be mindful of the tax implications of their real estate investments.

Global Implications

The growth of India's real estate market has attracted both domestic and global investors, driven by the country's economic expansion and the under-penetration of various real estate asset classes. This influx of investment is expected to continue, contributing significantly to the economy.

The evolution of real estate investment strategies in India, marked by the introduction of REITs and crowdfunding platforms, has significantly altered the investment landscape. These modern vehicles offer pathways to income generation and capital appreciation, making real estate investment more accessible, liquid, and diversified. As the Indian economy grows, these strategies are poised to channel more investments into the real estate sector, benefiting both individual investors and the broader economy.

The investment landscape has undergone a dramatic transformation, thanks in large part to the expansion of global markets and the advent of digital platforms. These developments have paved new paths for investors to diversify their portfolios, spreading risk more effectively while seizing emerging opportunities.

Global Market Diversification

Investing across different geographical regions has become increasingly accessible and is a key strategy for those looking to mitigate risks linked to domestic markets. The essence of global market diversification lies in its ability to cushion the blow of local economic downturns, political instability, or currency fluctuations. Since markets in various countries often move independently of each other, a dip in one region could be offset by growth in another, stabilizing overall portfolio performance.

Emerging markets, including countries like China, India, and Brazil, play a crucial role in this strategy. Their rapid economic growth presents attractive investment opportunities, though it's crucial to remember that these markets can also present higher volatility and risk.

Digital Platforms and Digital Real Estate

Digital platforms have revolutionized investment access and management, allowing for seamless diversification across asset classes, including stocks, bonds, and commodities. These platforms facilitate portfolio management with features like automatic rebalancing and asset allocation, making diversification more straightforward than ever.

Digital real estate, including domain names and online platforms, emerges as an innovative asset class, offering revenue generation through advertising and e-commerce. The global and scalable nature of digital investments breaks through traditional geographical barriers, offering unique growth prospects.

Strategies for Portfolio Diversification

Asset-Class Diversification: Spreading investments across various asset classes helps mitigate risk, as different assets react differently to market shifts.

Sector Diversification: Investing in diverse sectors safeguards against sector-specific downturns, with different sectors thriving under varying economic conditions.

Geographic Diversification: Investments in international markets can reduce the impact of local economic challenges while tapping into the growth potential of emerging economies.

Digital Real Estate: Digital assets offer a new dimension of diversification, capitalizing on the digital economy's expansion.

Time-Horizon Diversification: Allocating investments based on different time horizons addresses liquidity needs and risk tolerance, balancing immediate requirements with long-term goals.

Risk Diversification: Aligning the portfolio with the investor's risk tolerance is essential, mixing high-risk and high-reward investments with stable, lower-return assets.

The broadening of diversification strategies through global markets and digital platforms offers investors unprecedented opportunities to manage risk and pursue growth. However, diving into emerging markets and digital assets requires diligent research and an understanding of the unique risks involved.

Learning from Financial Leaders and Their Paths to Success

Warren Buffett, celebrated for his unparalleled success in the investment world as the chairman and CEO of Berkshire Hathaway, champions a value investing strategy that meticulously seeks out undervalued companies boasting strong fundamentals. This methodology is deeply influenced by Benjamin Graham's teachings, the father of value investing, yet is honed by Buffett's decades of investment experience and insight.

Intrinsic Value and Margin of Safety

Central to Buffett's investment philosophy is the pursuit of a company's intrinsic value - its true worth based on assets, earnings, dividends, and potential for growth, rather than its current market price. Buffett's goal is to acquire stocks at prices significantly lower than their intrinsic value, establishing a "margin of safety." This concept is crucial, as it offers a buffer against losses should the market conditions shift unfavorably or if the initial valuation proves incorrect.

Long-Term Perspective

Buffett is distinguished by his long-term view of investments, famously stating, "Our favorite holding period is forever." This long-term perspective allows him to overlook short-term market fluctuations, concentrating instead on the company's potential for value creation over an extended period. This philosophy underscores the significance of compounding returns, a key element in Buffett's investment success.

Quality Businesses with Economic Moats

A preference for investing in high-quality businesses that possess durable competitive advantages, or "economic moats," is another hallmark of Buffett's strategy. These moats might include superior brand recognition, proprietary technology, exclusive licenses, or a dominant market position, enabling these companies to maintain profitability and fend off competitors over the long haul.

Strong Management

For Buffett, a company's management quality is paramount. He looks for leaders who demonstrate integrity, astuteness in business, and an ownership mindset. Buffett understands that even the most promising business can flounder under poor leadership, whereas exceptional management can guide a company through tough times.

Financial Health and Performance

Buffett examines a company's financial statements to assess its performance and financial stability. He favors companies that show consistent earnings growth, high returns on equity (ROE), and robust free cash flow. He also advocates for low debt levels, as excessive borrowing can threaten a company's financial security.

Understandable Businesses

Sticking to investments within his "circle of competence," Buffett invests only in businesses he thoroughly understands. This principle ensures he can make well-informed decisions about a company's future prospects and the industry it operates in.

Valuation Metrics

While Buffett doesn't rely exclusively on conventional valuation metrics, he considers them in his analysis. Metrics like price-to-earnings (P/E) ratios, price-to-book (P/B) ratios, and dividend yields help him gauge whether a company's market price aligns with its intrinsic value.

Patience and Discipline

Buffett's approach is characterized by exceptional patience and discipline. He waits for the opportune moment to buy stocks at a discount to their intrinsic value and avoids following market trends or fads. This disciplined approach prevents overpaying for assets during market highs and positions him to capitalize on opportunities during downturns.

Warren Buffett's value investing strategy is a multifaceted approach that marries intrinsic value assessment with a thorough analysis of a company's long-term potential, competitive edge, financial health, and management quality. His disciplined, patient, and informed approach to investing, coupled with a focus on businesses within his understanding, has cemented his legacy as one of history's most successful investors.

Ray Dalio, renowned for founding Bridgewater Associates, the world's largest hedge fund, has long championed the power of diversification in investing. His creation, the "All Weather Portfolio," embodies this principle, crafted to withstand a range of economic conditions without the need to predict market directions. This portfolio, alongside Dalio's broader investment philosophy, provides crucial lessons for individual investors aiming for long-term wealth growth.

Understanding the All Weather Portfolio

The All Weather Portfolio is built on the premise that it's possible to design a portfolio resilient enough to endure any economic climate—whether facing inflation, deflation, rising or falling economic growth. Its asset allocation is meticulously structured to balance the risk-return profiles of different asset classes in response to the four primary economic scenarios that influence asset prices. The typical composition includes 55% bonds, 30% stocks, and 15% commodities and gold, based on historical performances of these asset classes under various economic conditions. For instance, while bonds have historically excelled during deflation or economic downturns, stocks have thrived in growth periods, with commodities and gold providing a hedge against inflation.

Dalio's Principles of Diversification

Dalio's investment strategy underlines "diversification" and "financial engineering" as cornerstones, emphasizing the significance of spreading investments across uncorrelated assets to diminish risk while potentially enhancing returns. He posits that through effective diversification, investors can significantly reduce their risk—by as much as 70% to 80%—without drastically impacting returns. This approach ensures that portfolios can smooth out the volatility of individual asset classes, yielding more stable and predictable returns over time.

Application for Individual Investors

Dalio's diversification principles offer several actionable insights for individual investors:

Embrace Broad Diversification: It's essential for investors to diversify across a wide spectrum of asset classes, including but not limited to stocks, bonds, commodities, and even alternative investments. This strategy helps shield the portfolio against significant losses in any one asset class.

Economic Cycles Insight: An understanding of how various economic cycles affect different asset classes can guide investors in fine-tuning their portfolios. However, the All Weather Portfolio's aim is to maintain a balanced asset allocation capable of weathering any economic condition without the need for constant adjustments.

Risk-Return Balance: Dalio advocates for concentrating on the return-to-risk ratio rather than merely chasing high returns. A well-diversified portfolio seeks to achieve the best possible returns for a given level of risk.

Leveraging Financial Engineering: This concept involves selecting diverse assets and combining them strategically to optimize the portfolio's overall risk and return. Thoughtful use of leverage to amplify returns on lower-risk investments can be part of this strategy.

Adopting a Long-Term Outlook: The All Weather Portfolio is designed with a decades-long horizon in mind. Individual investors are encouraged to adopt this long-term perspective, focusing on consistent growth over time rather than being swayed by short-term market movements.

Ray Dalio's All Weather Portfolio and his principles of diversification offer a solid framework for individual investors seeking sustainable wealth accumulation. By incorporating these strategies—broad diversification, insights into economic cycles, a balanced approach to risk and return, strategic financial engineering, and a long-term perspective—investors can construct resilient portfolios that are well-equipped to handle the uncertainties of the financial markets.

Cathie Wood, the driving force behind Ark Invest, has become synonymous with investing in disruptive innovation. Her strategy zeroes in on the potential of cutting-edge technologies like artificial intelligence, robotics, energy storage, DNA sequencing, and blockchain to radically alter industries and society. For individual investors looking to tap into the growth of innovative companies, Wood's approach offers a roadmap to identifying and capitalizing on future technological trends.

Cathie Wood's Investment Philosophy

Wood centers her investment strategy on disruptive innovation, a term she uses to describe technology-driven products or services with the power to redefine global markets. She posits that such breakthroughs can lead to significant market growth as they foster industry-wide transformations.

Key Areas of Focus

Ark Invest directs its attention towards five critical innovation areas:

Artificial Intelligence (AI): With its vast applications across sectors, AI is predicted to become a $80 trillion market within a decade.

Robotics: Adaptive robotics that can collaborate with humans is seen as a key growth area.

Energy Storage: The shift towards electric vehicles and renewable energy underscores the importance of advancements in energy storage.

DNA Sequencing: This technology is poised to revolutionize healthcare through personalized medicine and the potential eradication of diseases.

Blockchain Technology: Blockchain's ability to streamline and secure financial transactions positions it as a foundational future technology.

Investment Strategy

Wood's strategy is to invest in companies leading these innovation sectors, focusing on those with exponential growth potential. Ark Invest actively manages its portfolios, aiming for long-term growth by backing disruptive leaders.

Takeaways for Individual Investors

Embrace Innovation: Consider the role of innovation in portfolio development. Investments in technology leaders can yield substantial returns as these entities reshape industries.

Research and Diversification: Comprehensive research is crucial to identifying promising innovations.

Diversification across innovative sectors mitigates risk while capturing varied growth opportunities.

Long-Term Perspective: Investing in innovation is inherently long-term. Patience is necessary as disruptive technologies evolve and reach their market potential, despite potential volatility.

Transparency and Education: Ark Invest's commitment to transparency, by sharing holdings and trades daily, highlights the importance of staying informed and understanding your investments.

Risk Management: The high-return potential of innovative investments comes with volatility. Align such investments with your risk tolerance and overall portfolio strategy.

Stay Informed: Keeping up with technological and market trends is essential. Wood's success stems from a deep understanding of how emerging technologies can impact the global economy.

Cathie Wood's emphasis on disruptive innovation outlines a strategy for individual investors to maximize wealth by leveraging technological advancements. Wood's investment philosophy underscores the significance of informed, forward-thinking investment strategies in achieving growth in the rapidly evolving landscape of disruptive innovation.

This exploration into the strategies of some of the most successful investors of our time reveals a common theme: the pursuit of growth through disciplined investment, diversification, and a keen eye for innovation. We've delved into the principles of investing in undervalued companies with strong fundamentals, spreading risk across various economic conditions, and placing bets on disruptive technologies poised for exponential growth. These approaches offer a roadmap for navigating the financial markets, emphasizing the importance of a long-term perspective, thorough research, and an adaptable strategy.

As individual investors, the lessons drawn from these investment philosophies empower us to make informed decisions, spot emerging trends, and build resilient portfolios capable of weathering market uncertainties. The journey through these investment strategies is a testament to the power of patience, the value of knowledge, and the potential of innovation in shaping our financial future.

In the words of John C. Bogle, "The stock market is a giant distraction to the business of investing." This quote encapsulates the essence of our exploration, reminding us to focus on the underlying principles of investment rather than being swayed by the market's fleeting movements. It encourages us to stay committed to our investment goals, guided by wisdom, strategy, and an unwavering focus on long-term growth.

Chapter 4

Beyond the Numbers

"Discipline is choosing between what you want now and what you want most."

–Abraham Lincoln.

Lincoln's profound viewpoint illuminates the core of financial discipline and patience, highlighting their pivotal importance in achieving financial objectives. Within the domain of personal finance, these virtues direct us towards lasting success and steering clear of the allure of immediate gratifications.

The Role of Discipline in Financial Success

Financial discipline is the foundation upon which lasting financial health is built. It's about making consistent, strategic choices that align with your future aspirations, rather than succumbing to the allure of immediate gratification. This disciplined approach enables individuals to prioritize their spending, saving, and investing in a way that moves them closer to their goals with each decision made.

The power of discipline lies in its ability to transform abstract goals into tangible outcomes. Whether it's saving for retirement, paying off debt, or building an emergency fund, discipline turns intention into action. It requires a commitment to a set of financial principles and practices that may sometimes demand sacrifice in the present for the sake of a more secure and prosperous future.

The Power of Patience in Achieving Financial Goals

Patience is the complementary force that, when combined with discipline, yields remarkable results in personal finance. It acknowledges that true financial growth doesn't happen overnight but is the result of compounded efforts over time. Patience is what allows investors to ride out the volatility of markets, savers to accumulate significant emergency funds, and debtors to steadily reduce their burdens without losing hope.

Moreover, patience cultivates a mindset of resilience. It helps individuals to see beyond the immediate fluctuations in their financial journey, focusing instead on the broader horizon of their long-term goals. This long view is crucial for making informed, deliberate financial decisions that are not swayed by the temporary highs and lows of the economic landscape.

Together, discipline and patience equip individuals with the tools necessary to navigate the complexities of personal finance. They underscore the importance of staying the course, making smart, forward-looking choices, and allowing time to work its magic on your investments and savings. In a world where instant gratification is often the norm, these virtues stand out as key differentiators between fleeting success and lasting financial well-being.

Creating a financial discipline plan is like setting your sails for a journey towards financial stability and growth. It offers a structured method to move through your financial life with deliberate intention and clear goals. Here's how to establish this foundation and progressively build on it:

Understand Your Current Financial State

The first step in cultivating financial discipline involves a deep dive into your current spending habits. Begin by meticulously tracking every transaction, whether through a traditional notebook, a spreadsheet, or a financial app. Categorize your expenditures into areas such as housing, utilities, groceries, dining out, and transportation. Over time, patterns will emerge, revealing perhaps an unexpected high expenditure on non-essentials like dining out or unused app subscriptions. Recognizing these trends is pivotal in identifying areas for adjustment.

Crafting a Budget

Armed with the insights from your spending analysis, the next step is to create a budget—a roadmap for your financial journey. The 50/30/20 plan offers a balanced approach: allocating 50% of your income to necessities, 30% to wants, and 20% to savings and debt repayment. This framework provides a starting point from which you can tailor a budget that suits your unique financial situation, directing your funds purposefully towards your priorities.

Automate to Prioritize Savings and Debt Repayment

To fortify your financial discipline, automate your savings contributions and debt repayments. This ensures that essential financial goals are not sidelined by impulsive spending. Automation acts as a safeguard, preventing late payments and fostering a savings culture that prepares you for unforeseen emergencies without resorting to credit.

Halting New Debt

The cycle of acquiring new debt often stems from undisciplined spending. To break this cycle, it's crucial to incorporate a discretionary spending allowance within your budget. This small, allocated amount allows for personal indulgences without derailing your financial plan. Additionally, instituting a cooling-off period for purchases—waiting at least a night before making a buy—can significantly reduce impulse spending, helping to curb the accumulation of new debt.

Regular Debt Monitoring

Even with automated repayments, staying informed about your debt levels is essential. Regularly, perhaps bi-weekly, reviewing your credit card, loan, and line of credit balances keeps you aware of your financial obligations and progress towards paying them off. This awareness is critical in maintaining financial discipline, as it reinforces the impact of every financial decision on your overall debt levels.

Cultivating Patience

Adapting to a disciplined financial lifestyle and achieving your goals is a gradual process. It's natural to face setbacks; however, patience is your ally. If you falter, refocus on the broader vision of financial independence and resilience. Remember, each step taken is progress, and with time, disciplined efforts will culminate in significant financial achievements.

The Marshmallow Test Applied To Finance

The Marshmallow Test, a seminal experiment from the late 1960s by Walter Mischel and his colleagues at Stanford

University, has become a foundational study in understanding delayed gratification. It illuminates individual differences in self-control and offers insights into how these differences influence broader societal behaviors and the challenges of modern life. This experiment's relevance extends into many areas, including personal finance, highlighting the importance of resisting immediate rewards to achieve long-term financial stability and success.

Implications for Personal Finance

In personal finance, the ability to delay gratification plays a pivotal role. The Marshmallow Test underscores a vital principle: those who can forego immediate pleasures for future rewards tend to enjoy greater financial security. This concept is especially pertinent in today's culture of consumer debt and instant gratification, where the discipline to invest in the future is both crucial and challenging. Adhering to this principle aids in avoiding debt, making informed investment decisions, and effectively planning for retirement.

Impact on Digital Consumption and Attention Spans

The digital era has intensified the challenge of delayed gratification. With round-the-clock access to various forms of digital content, the lure of immediate gratification is stronger than ever. This constant connectivity can diminish attention spans and foster a preference for short, fleeting content, making it harder to engage with more substantial, meaningful material. The Marshmallow Test's insights into self-control are particularly relevant here, shedding light on behaviors linked to social media use and other digital interactions.

Educational Outcomes and Learning Processes

The capacity for delayed gratification is also tied to academic achievement. Children who demonstrate the ability to wait for larger rewards tend to have better educational outcomes over time. This connection suggests that nurturing patience and self-control from an early age can yield significant benefits within educational settings. Yet, the current focus on quick results and standardized testing often neglects the development of these critical skills, pointing to the need for an educational approach that values long-term effort and patience.

Societal and Economic Inequalities

Further, the Marshmallow Test highlights how socioeconomic factors influence the ability to delay gratification. Children from less stable or economically disadvantaged backgrounds may struggle more with holding out for future rewards, reflecting wider societal and economic disparities. This observation calls for targeted policies and initiatives that help bridge these gaps, ensuring every individual has the chance to develop the skills necessary for future success.

Strategies for Enhancing Delayed Gratification

To cultivate the ability to delay gratification, individuals can employ various strategies. Setting clear, realistic goals, adhering to a budget aligned with long-term objectives, and seeking alternative ways to satisfy immediate desires can all enhance self-control. Additionally, a deeper understanding of the psychological underpinnings of impulse control can empower individuals to make decisions that favor their future well-being.

The Marshmallow Test provides valuable lessons on human behavior and its implications across life's many facets, from managing finances to navigating the digital world, achieving educational success, and addressing social inequalities. Embracing the principles of delayed gratification allows for decisions that lead to a more fulfilling and prosperous life. As we move forward, the challenge of prioritizing long-term benefits over immediate temptations remains ever-present, highlighting the continued importance of developing and fostering self-control in pursuit of long-term goals.

Reflecting on the lessons from the Marshmallow Test has significantly shaped my approach to financial planning and decision-making. Through my journey, I've discovered the profound impact that patience and discipline can have on achieving long-term financial stability and success.

One of the first steps I took was to rigorously apply the concept of delayed gratification to my spending habits. In a world where the next purchase is just a click away, resisting the allure of immediate satisfaction was challenging but essential. I started by setting specific, long-term financial goals, such as building an emergency fund, saving for a down payment on a home, and contributing more aggressively to my retirement accounts. The vision of these goals served as a powerful motivator, helping me navigate past short-term desires in favor of long-term financial health.

Automation played a crucial role in reinforcing my financial discipline. By setting up automatic transfers to savings and investment accounts, I removed the temptation and emotional bias from the equation. This ensured that a portion of my income was consistently allocated towards my financial goals and helped inculcate a sense of discipline in managing my finances. Watching my savings grow over time, albeit slowly, was both rewarding and affirming, reinforcing the value of patience in the journey towards financial independence.

The journey was not without its setbacks. There were moments when the lure of instant gratification won over my resolve, leading to purchases that I later regretted. However, instead of viewing these lapses as failures, I saw them as learning opportunities. They served as reminders of the importance of maintaining focus on my financial objectives and the need for continuous self-discipline.

Balancing Ambition with Contentment

Balancing ambition with contentment in the context of personal finance requires a nuanced understanding of what truly matters to you, beyond the noise of societal expectations. This balance isn't about settling but finding harmony between striving for more and appreciating what you already have. Here are exercises designed to help delineate your personal definitions of financial success and contentment, ensuring they reflect your values and aspirations, not just external benchmarks.

Visualize Your Ideal Financial Life

Starting your journey toward financial well-being begins with a clear vision of your destination. It's not merely about gathering wealth; it's about crafting a life that embodies your core values and dreams. Picture, in the peacefulness of your own space, your ideal financial scenario. Is it the liberty to chase your passions without the worry of funds, the chance to traverse and immerse in different cultures, or the comfort of a well-stocked retirement nest?

Visualize the daily joys that come with this financial liberty: waking free from the chains of debt, cherishing moments with loved ones without the shadow of bills, or the excitement of an adventure once deemed too extravagant. Let the feelings these visions stir within you—contentment, peace, exhilaration—be the bedrock of your financial ambitions. This exercise in visualization brings your goals within reach and crafts a compelling narrative that inspires the journey ahead, driven by the powerful emotions linked to your financial dreams.

Create a "Contentment List"

In the pursuit of financial goals, it's easy to overlook the wealth already present in your life. Creating a "Contentment List" is an exercise in recognizing and cherishing the aspects of your current financial situation that contribute to your happiness. Start by jotting down the financial freedoms you currently enjoy, no matter how small they might seem. Perhaps it's the simple pleasure of a subscription service that brings you joy, the financial stability to indulge in a favorite hobby, or the reassurance that comes from having an emergency fund.

Review and update this list regularly to remind yourself of the progress you've made and the blessings you currently enjoy. This practice fosters a sense of gratitude and contentment, serving as a counterbalance to the endless pursuit of more. It helps differentiate between the pursuit of happiness through material gains and the genuine contentment that comes from appreciating what you have. In distinguishing needs from wants, you'll find that true happiness often lies in the freedoms and experiences that financial stability brings, rather than in the accumulation of possessions.

The Aspiration Gap Analysis

The Aspiration Gap Analysis involves a straightforward yet profound exercise that bridges the gap between where you are and where you wish to be financially. Start by listing your top three financial goals. These could range from buying a home, achieving a certain level of savings, to starting your own business. Alongside these goals, note three aspects of your current financial life that bring you satisfaction. This dual perspective fosters an appreciation for your current achievements while maintaining focus on future aspirations.

For each goal, outline the actionable steps required to move closer to realization. Perhaps achieving a certain savings target necessitates cutting back on discretionary spending or seeking additional income sources. Recognize that each step towards a goal may require certain sacrifices or trade-offs. For instance, redirecting funds from leisure expenses to investment accounts. This analysis illuminates the path forward and ensures that the pursuit of future aspirations does not overshadow present contentment.

The "Why" Deep Dive

The "Why" Deep Dive is a reflective exercise designed to peel back the layers of your financial goals, revealing the core motivations that drive them. Begin with a simple goal, like purchasing a luxury car, and continuously ask "Why?" until you reach the fundamental reason behind this aspiration. This iterative questioning might reveal that the desire for a luxury car is less about the vehicle itself and more about the sense of achievement or status it represents.

This introspection can lead to surprising revelations about what truly motivates our financial decisions. It might unveil a deeper quest for security, recognition, or happiness, which could be fulfilled in ways other than acquiring material possessions. Understanding these underlying motivations allows for a more authentic alignment of financial goals with personal values and desires, ensuring that the pursuit of financial success enriches your life in meaningful ways.

Set "Enough" Benchmarks

Define what "enough" looks like in different areas of your financial life, such as savings, income, or investments. These benchmarks should represent points at which your needs and reasonable wants are met, providing a buffer against the perpetual pursuit of more. Recognizing these points can foster a sense of contentment and prevent the trap of endlessly chasing more without appreciating what you've achieved.

These exercises are designed to bring clarity and personal insight into what financial success and contentment mean to you. By focusing on personal values and intrinsic motivations, you can create a financial path that is both ambitious and fulfilling, tailored to your unique life and aspirations. This approach encourages a healthier relationship with money, one where financial decisions are driven by a clear understanding of what truly contributes to your personal well-being and happiness.

In the pursuit of financial goals, it's easy to get caught up in what's next, often overlooking the milestones we've already achieved. Appreciating your current achievements while ambitiously striving for more is a delicate balance. Techniques like gratitude journaling and savoring exercises specifically tailored to financial milestones can significantly enhance this balance, making the journey as rewarding as the destination. Here's how to integrate these practices into your financial planning:

Gratitude Journaling Tailored to Financial Achievements

Gratitude journaling, a well-regarded practice for enhancing overall well-being, can be specifically adapted to focus on financial accomplishments. Start by dedicating a notebook or digital document to your financial journey. Regularly, perhaps weekly or monthly, take time to reflect on and write down financial achievements you're thankful for. These entries could range from sticking to your budget, making a significant payment towards debt, or reaching a savings goal.

The act of writing reinforces the positive emotions associated with these achievements, fostering a sense of progress and contentment. Over time, reviewing this journal can offer perspective, reminding you of how far you've come and motivating you to continue striving for your goals. This practice encourages a mindset that values and recognizes growth, no matter the scale.

Savoring Exercises for Financial Milestones

Savoring is the practice of consciously engaging with and appreciating the positive aspects of experiences. Applying this to financial milestones involves taking deliberate time to celebrate and reflect on the significance of these achievements. For example, when you reach a savings goal, instead of immediately setting the next target, pause to savor this accomplishment. You might celebrate with a small, meaningful reward or simply spend a moment acknowledging the effort and discipline it took to get there.

Creating rituals around financial milestones can also enhance the savoring experience. For instance, you could have a special dinner, a quiet evening reflecting on your journey, or a family gathering to mark the achievement. The key is to associate positive, memorable experiences with financial progress, reinforcing the motivation to continue pursuing your goals.

Integrating Gratitude and Savoring into Financial Planning

Integrating these techniques into your financial planning involves making them regular practices. Schedule time for gratitude journaling and plan how you'll celebrate future financial milestones. As you incorporate these practices, they become part of your financial strategy, ensuring that appreciation and enjoyment are woven into the fabric of your financial journey.

Moreover, sharing your achievements and gratitude practices with loved ones can amplify the positive effects. It provides accountability and creates an environment where financial progress is collectively recognized and celebrated.

As we wrap up this chapter, I want to share a thought with you, one that's grown clearer with every word we've explored together. This journey we're on, figuring out our finances, isn't just about filling spreadsheets or watching numbers climb.

It's about understanding ourselves, our desires, and how we respond to the world around us. It's about realizing that every decision we make, financial or otherwise, reflects who we are and what we value most. The exercises and insights we've delved into are tools, yes, but they're also mirrors, reflecting back the complexity, challenges, and joys of striving for a life that's rich in more ways than one.

Chapter 5
Creating your Wealth Ecosystem

"Your network is your net worth." This phrase, often attributed to Porter Gale, resonates profoundly when we think about financial success as a culmination of the relationships we nurture. In my journey, I've come to realize that networking is a strategic tool for gathering financial wisdom, discovering opportunities, and building a support system that can significantly accelerate the path to wealth maximization.

Networking in the context of financial success involves more than casual interactions; it requires a deliberate approach to identify and engage with people who can shed light on financial strategies, investments, and economic trends. This could mean connecting with financial advisors, successful investors, or industry experts who offer perspectives that challenge and refine your financial understanding.

Start by defining what financial success looks like for you. Is it achieving early retirement, building a diverse investment portfolio, or becoming a savvy real estate investor? Your goals shape whom you should seek out.

Engagement goes beyond passive observation. It involves asking thoughtful questions, sharing your insights, and offering help where you can. This two-way exchange enriches your understanding and strengthens your relationships within the financial community. When reaching out directly to potential mentors or peers, be specific about what aspects of their work interest you and what you hope to learn from them. Genuine curiosity and a willingness to engage in meaningful dialogue can pave the way for deeper connections.

While digital platforms offer convenience, the value of face-to-face interactions remains unparalleled. Attend financial seminars, workshops, and meetups in your area. These gatherings provide a unique opportunity to connect with like-minded individuals, share experiences, and learn from successful practitioners in the field. The personal connections made in these settings often lead to mentorships, partnerships, and friendships that are invaluable in your financial journey.

The insights and opportunities garnered through networking can dramatically influence your financial decisions and strategies. For instance, a casual conversation at a networking event might introduce you to the concept of index fund investing, changing the way you approach your investment portfolio. Or, a mentor met through an online forum could provide guidance on dealing with the complexities of rental property investment, saving you from potential pitfalls.

Networking Strategies for Financial Success

Networking for financial success is about curating a community of individuals who inspire you, challenge you, and support you. It's a reminder that while wealth creation might seem like a solitary endeavor, it is deeply enriched by the collective wisdom and encouragement of those we choose to connect with.

Forging meaningful connections is as essential as your technical expertise in the financial. Let's delve into practical strategies for leveraging relationships that pave the way to financial mastery and wealth maximization. Here's a closer look at how you can harness these opportunities to their fullest potential:

Leverage Local Events and Conferences

Immerse yourself in finance-related events, conferences, and seminars that span the length and breadth of India. These venues are arenas where the future of finance is debated, shaped, and driven forward. By actively engaging in discussions and workshops, you don't merely attend; you contribute to the conversation, shining a light on your expertise. Picture this: presenting a case study at a seminar in Mumbai on emerging market trends, sparking a discussion that later transitions to a collaborative project with industry leaders. Such active participation can open doors to collaborations and opportunities previously unseen.

Join Professional Associations

Membership in professional associations like the Association of Financial Planners (AFP) India or the Indian Association of Investment Professionals (IAIP) serves as a source for continuous learning and networking. These organizations are about being part of a community committed to professional excellence. Through regular meetings, webinars, and newsletters, you stay abreast of industry trends, regulatory changes, and opportunities for professional development. Imagine being part of a panel discussion organized by the IAIP, where you share insights on portfolio management strategies post-pandemic, positioning yourself as an authority in your field.

Utilize Digital Platforms

In today's digital age, platforms like LinkedIn have become indispensable for professionals across the globe, including India. But it's not just about having a presence; it's about being actively engaged. Joining finance-specific groups such as "Finance Professionals India" or "Indian Financial Market" on LinkedIn allows you to dive deep into discussions, share your articles or insights, and connect with peers and mentors. This digital engagement extends your professional network beyond geographic boundaries, establishing your reputation as a knowledgeable and insightful finance professional.

Cultivate Relationships with Alumni Networks

Alumni networks, particularly from institutions like the Indian Institutes of Management (IIMs) or the Indian School of Business (ISB), are treasure troves of opportunity. These networks often host events and online forums where you can engage with both peers and industry veterans. For example, participating in an alumni-led webinar on emerging financial technologies broadens your knowledge and puts you in direct contact with alumni who are at the forefront of finance innovation. Such platforms can serve as a springboard for collaborations or mentorship.

Connect with Industry Leaders

Reaching out to industry leaders for informational interviews is a strategic move. Imagine emailing a CEO of a leading fintech startup with a concise message expressing admiration for their work and requesting a short meeting to discuss industry trends. Such interactions can be enlightening, providing you with firsthand insights into the challenges and opportunities within the sector. The advice and perspectives garnered from these meetings can guide your career trajectory in unexpected and rewarding ways.

Engage in Community Service

Community service, especially in initiatives aimed at financial literacy and inclusion, aligns you with individuals and organizations committed to making a difference. Volunteering for a financial literacy workshop in rural areas, for instance, contributes to societal welfare and connects you with professionals who share a vision of inclusive financial growth. These connections often lead to collaborations that are both fulfilling and professionally enriching.

Build a Local Presence

In cities like Mumbai, Bangalore, Delhi, and Hyderabad, attending regional networking events and joining local business clubs puts you in the midst of India's financial activity. Being part of a local business meetup can introduce you to potential clients, partners, or mentors. The personal connections made in these settings can be more impactful than online interactions, leading to stronger professional relationships.

Explore Mentorship Opportunities

Seeking mentorship from experienced finance professionals can significantly accelerate your learning curve. Whether it's through formal mentorship programs or informal relationships, the guidance received from a mentor is invaluable. Consider approaching a potential mentor with a specific request for guidance on a project or decision. This shows initiative and provides a clear context for the mentor to assist you.

Attend Informal Social Gatherings

Informal social gatherings, such as industry mixers or casual meet-ups, offer a relaxed environment to connect with peers and leaders. These settings often facilitate deeper conversations and a chance to know professionals on a personal level. Sharing a meal or a coffee can lead to discussions about shared interests, challenges, and opportunities, laying the groundwork for strong professional bonds.

Collaborate on Financial Projects

Working on financial projects or research with peers exemplifies your commitment to the field and willingness to engage in collective problem-solving. This collaboration could be as formal as co-authoring a research paper on market trends or as informal as organizing a study group for financial certification exams. Such initiatives enhance your knowledge and demonstrate your leadership and teamwork skills.

Utilize Financial Technology Communities

India's burgeoning fintech sector is ripe with innovation. Engaging with fintech communities, whether through online forums, social media, or attending fintech startup events, keeps you at the cutting edge of the industry. Participation in a hackathon or a fintech innovation challenge, for example, can connect you with forward-thinking entrepreneurs and technologists, opening doors to potential collaborations or investments.

Follow Up and Nurture Relationships

Consistency in follow-up after meetings and events is key to nurturing professional relationships. A personalized email or message appreciating the conversation and suggesting a future touchpoint can make a lasting impression. Sharing an article or report that you discussed during your meeting shows attentiveness and fosters a continued exchange of ideas.

Offer Value Before Expecting It

Providing assistance, sharing knowledge, or making introductions without immediate expectation of return cultivates goodwill and establishes you as a valuable member of the financial community. Offering to help a peer with a financial model or introducing a contact to a potential investor without soliciting anything in return can significantly enhance your reputation and network.

By adopting these strategies, you position yourself as a participant in India's financial sector, but as a contributor to its growth and dynamism. Each interaction is an opportunity to learn, share, and build towards a mutually prosperous future.

The Importance of Mentorship and Community in Financial Education

Finding the right mentor in finance, someone who can genuinely guide you toward achieving your financial goals, is more than just ticking boxes on a list of qualifications. It's about connecting with someone who gets where you want to go and knows how to help you get there. Here's a practical take on what to look for in a financial mentor:

Relevant Experience and Expertise

If you're keen on mastering investments, you'd benefit from a mentor who's been in the trenches of investing and has also come out ahead. Their journey through ups and downs becomes a rich source of real-world advice for you. It's like having a guide who knows the map by heart because they've walked the path themselves.

Alignment with Financial Goals

Your mentor should get your financial dreams—be it financial independence, saving for a big life event, or building wealth through smart investments. This shared vision means their advice will be directly applicable to your journey, not generic counsel that you could find in any finance book or blog.

Teaching and Communication Skills

The best knowledge in the world won't help much if your mentor can't share it in a way that makes sense to you. Look for someone patient and clear, who can break down complex financial jargon into simple, actionable advice. It's like finding that one teacher who could make even the driest subject come alive in class.

Ethical Standards and Integrity

Trust is non-negotiable. You want a mentor who places your interests first, without any hidden agendas. Their advice should be transparent and unbiased, guided by high ethical standards. It's reassuring to know that the guidance you're getting is both honest and in your best interest.

Availability and Commitment

A mentor willing to invest their time in your growth is crucial. This doesn't mean they need to be on call 24/7, but there should be a commitment to regular check-ins and updates. It's about having that go-to person who's there to support, challenge, and push you toward your financial goals.

Personal Rapport

Finally, the chemistry needs to be right. You'll be sharing your financial life with this person, so feeling comfortable and connected is key. It's about finding that mentor who doesn't just see numbers but understands your aspirations and challenges on a personal level.

Here's a practical roadmap to approaching a mentor who can be instrumental in your financial growth:

Prepare Your Approach

Before reaching out, take a moment to crystallize your objectives. What exactly are you looking to gain from this mentorship? Pin down your financial goals and the areas you need guidance in. This clarity will help you in articulating your needs and in demonstrating your seriousness and preparedness to potential mentors.

Initial Contact

The first message you send is your virtual handshake. Whether it's through email or LinkedIn, your introduction should be succinct yet compelling. Explain why you admire their work and specify what you hope to learn from them. Suggesting a brief conversation to explore the possibility of mentorship shows respect for their time and opens the door for further dialogue.

Build a Relationship

Trust and rapport are the cornerstones of any mentorship. Use your first meeting not just to pitch your goals but to engage in a genuine two-way conversation. Understanding their perspective, experience, and mentoring style is crucial to gauging compatibility. Remember, mentorship is a two-way street; ensuring a good fit is as much about their willingness to invest in you as it is about your readiness to learn.

Set Clear Expectations

Once the mentorship wheels are in motion, it's time to lay down the framework of your relationship. Discuss the logistics—how often you'll meet, preferred communication channels, and what you both aim to achieve. Clear expectations are the bedrock of a fruitful mentorship, ensuring both mentor and mentee are aligned and committed to the journey ahead.

Approaching a potential financial mentor with respect, clarity, and a genuine desire for growth paves the way for a mentorship rich in learning and personal development. This relationship can become one of the most influential factors in your quest for financial mastery, offering knowledge and the confidence to make informed decisions on your path to wealth maximization.

Finding your own way through financial education can sometimes feel overwhelming, especially when you're striving to achieve wealth maximization. Whether it's deciphering investment strategies or understanding market trends, the journey is always easier—and more enriching—when you're not going it alone. Joining or starting financial education groups offers a communal path to learning, growth, and success. Here's how you can dive into this world, making the most of both existing groups and possibly starting your own.

Joining Existing Financial Education Groups

Online Communities and Forums

Start your exploration by diving into online platforms rich in financial education. Websites and forums dedicated to personal finance, especially those with a focus on the Indian market, are invaluable. Engage actively in these communities by asking questions, sharing insights, and participating in discussions. This active participation enhances your learning and connects you with mentors and peers who can guide your journey.

Local Meetups and Workshops

Look for local finance groups on platforms like Meetup. com, which often host events ranging from investor meetups to financial literacy workshops. Regular attendance and participation in these groups provide a solid foundation for practical knowledge and peer discussion. Contributing to these communities, perhaps by sharing your own experiences or leading a discussion, cements your status within the group and deepens your understanding of complex financial concepts.

Starting Your Own Financial Education Group

If existing groups don't meet your needs or if you're inspired to lead, starting your own financial education group can be a fulfilling endeavor.

Define the Group's Purpose and Structure

Clarify what you want your group to achieve. Will it focus on general financial education, delve into specific investment strategies, or explore niche areas of personal finance? Deciding on the structure is also crucial—whether it's an informal gathering for knowledge exchange or a formal investment club.

Recruit Members

Start building your community by reaching out to interested friends, family, and colleagues. Utilizing social media and online forums can help attract a diverse group of members. It's important to establish clear membership criteria that align with the group's goals and structure.

Organize Meetings and Activities

Plan regular meetings to ensure a steady flow of discussion, learning, and collaboration. Crafting an agenda for each meeting helps keep discussions focused, allowing time for educational segments, investment analysis, or member questions.

Provide Resources and Education

Aim to offer a wealth of educational materials to your group members, from curated articles and books to online courses. Encouraging members to lead discussions or present on topics diversifies the learning experience and helps each member grow in confidence and knowledge.

Utilize Technology

Embrace digital tools to enhance communication and collaboration within your group. Online platforms can facilitate discussions, while shared documents and spreadsheets aid in organizing and tracking group activities and resources. Creating an online presence for your group, like a website or social media page, can also attract new members and serve as a platform for sharing financial knowledge more widely.

Whether you're joining existing groups or starting your own, the key is to engage actively and contribute meaningally. This journey is about building a community where knowledge, experiences, and successes are shared, creating a collective path to financial empowerment.

Building and Maintaining a Personal Brand That Attracts Opportunities

Personal branding transforms your professional journey into a guiding light, bringing more opportunities your way. It's about showcasing who you are, what you stand for, and the unique blend of skills you bring to the table. This strategic self-presentation does wonders for your financial growth, letting your authentic self attract the wealth and opportunities you seek. Here's how personal branding makes a tangible impact:

Building Credibility and Trust

Imagine your personal brand as a bridge connecting you to potential clients, investors, and partners. This bridge is built on your visible achievements, expertise, and the values you embody. When people see your journey, your challenges, and how you've overcome them, they see a leader they can trust. This trust is the foundation of fruitful, long-lasting professional relationships.

Distinguishing Yourself

In the vast sea of professionals, your personal brand is the lighthouse that makes you visible. It's about more than your job title; it's the narrative you create around your experiences and how you approach problems. This uniqueness makes you the person of choice for projects and roles that fit precisely with what you offer.

Cultivating a Loyal Following

Sharing your knowledge and insights does more than educate; it connects. Through blogs, social media, or speaking engagements, when you open up about your professional passions or the lessons you've learned, you're resonating with people. This resonance builds a community around your brand, a community that's eager to support your ventures.

Amplifying Visibility

Using platforms like LinkedIn or Twitter effectively turns your personal brand into a global voice. This visibility ensures your name comes up in conversations about your field, opening up opportunities for collaboration, speaking engagements, and more. Each post you share, each insight you offer, adds another layer to your brand, making it richer and more attractive to potential collaborators.

Opening Career Doors

Your personal brand paves the way for career evolution. It's a dynamic showcase of your growth, adaptability, and readiness for new challenges. As you go through your career, your brand evolves, highlighting your journey towards greater achievements and readiness for more significant opportunities.

Strengthening Negotiation

A strong personal brand gives you leverage in negotiations. It's a testament to your value, helping you secure better contracts, higher salaries, and more favorable conditions. Your brand's strength lies in the perceived value you bring to the table, empowering you to ask for what you're worth.

Generating Multiple Revenue Streams

Personal branding enables you to monetize your expertise in diverse ways. Whether it's writing a book, launching courses, or speaking at conferences, these channels provide immediate financial benefits and contribute to a sustainable, long-term income.

Your personal brand is the sum total of your professional life, distilled into a narrative that's both compelling and uniquely yours. It's about leveraging your authentic self to attract the opportunities and connections that drive financial success. In the context of wealth maximization, a well-cultivated personal brand is your most valuable asset.

Cultivating a powerful personal brand and network is equivalent to tending a garden. You start by planting seeds of connection and knowledge, then diligently nurture them to watch them flourish and yield results. My own path has demonstrated the accuracy of this metaphor, showing that persistent effort and smart engagement are crucial. Below are some effective strategies I've discovered that you can tailor to enhance your own path toward establishing a personal brand that can be leveraged for maximizing wealth:

Regular Updates and Communication

- **Stay Active on Social Media:** Platforms like LinkedIn, Twitter, and Instagram are stages for your professional narrative. By regularly posting updates, sharing insights, and engaging with your audience, you keep your brand alive in the minds of your followers. Tailoring your content to fit each platform maximizes your reach and impact.

- **Newsletter Distribution:** A newsletter is a direct line to your network, allowing you to share industry news, personal milestones, and professional insights. It positions you as a knowledgeable leader, keeping your audience connected and informed.

- **Content Creation:** Writing blog posts or articles on industry-relevant topics showcases your expertise. Sharing these pieces enriches your network and cements your status as a thought leader.

- **Personal Achievements:** Don't shy away from sharing your successes. Every achievement, be it a promotion, a certification, or a project victory, is a testament to your growth and capability.

Engaging with Your Community

- **Interactive Events:** Hosting webinars or workshops encourages active participation and strengthens community bonds. It's a dynamic way to share knowledge and interact directly with your audience.

- **Community Involvement:** Engaging in projects that resonate with your brand values demonstrates a commitment to broader causes, enriching your personal brand with depth and sincerity.
- **Member-Generated Content:** Inviting your community to contribute content fosters a collaborative spirit, making your network a lively, engaging space.
- **Responsive Interaction:** Being prompt and thoughtful in your responses to comments and messages shows you value and respect your community's input and engagement.

Offering Value to Your Connections

- **Share Knowledge:** Consistently providing your network with actionable advice and resources enables growth and amplifies your influence as a trusted advisor.
- **Mentorship and Support:** Offering guidance or support to others aids their development and expands your sphere of influence, enriching your network with diverse perspectives and opportunities.
- **Networking Events:** Participating in networking events exposes you to new connections and ideas, further expanding your professional landscape.
- **Collaborations:** Partnering with other professionals opens up avenues for mutual growth, allowing both parties to tap into each other's networks.

Staying Relevant

- **Continuous Learning:** Keeping abreast of industry trends and developments ensures your knowledge remains current, reinforcing your brand's relevance and authority.

- **Adapt to Change:** Embracing change and innovating your approach reflect a forward-thinking mindset, crucial for staying ahead in a rapidly evolving market.
- **Feedback and Adaptation:** Seeking and acting on feedback demonstrates a commitment to continuous improvement, making your brand resilient and responsive.
- **Personal Brand Refinement:** As you evolve, so should your brand. Regularly revisiting and refining your brand ensures it accurately reflects your current expertise and aspirations.

In the journey of wealth maximization, your personal brand and network are invaluable assets. Like a garden, they require regular care, strategic nurturing, and an open, adaptive approach to flourish. Through dedicated engagement and continuous growth, you can transform your personal brand into a dynamic force that propels you toward your financial goals.

Stumbling upon an article about Gary Vaynerchuk on LinkedIn was a serendipitous moment for me. It detailed how he leveraged his unmistakable personal brand to navigate the business world and to carve out a vast empire that spans several industries. The more I delved into his story, the more I realized the unmatched power of authentic personal branding in wealth maximization. Here's a closer look at Gary Vee's journey and the strategies that anyone can draw inspiration from.

Gary Vee began his entrepreneurial journey in his family's wine business, but it was the launch of Wine Library TV, a webcast dedicated to wine, that marked the birth of his personal brand. His approach—knowledgeable yet incredibly direct and genuine—resonated with viewers far beyond the wine community.

Strategies Used

Content Creation and Social Media Mastery: Gary's early recognition of content and social media's potential allowed him to connect with a global audience. His authenticity and engagement on platforms from Twitter to TikTok became a masterclass in building a following.

Diversification of Ventures: Using his growing personal brand, Gary expanded his reach by founding VaynerMedia and VaynerSports. His brand's strength attracted clients and partners, diversifying his business interests and revenue streams.

Thought Leadership: Gary established himself as a go-to expert in digital marketing and entrepreneurship. His insights, shared through books and talks, cemented his reputation, drawing in more opportunities.

Direct Engagement with Audience: Known for his unparalleled interaction with followers, Gary's responsiveness and engagement have built a community of loyal fans and customers, crucial for any brand's longevity.

Impact on Wealth Maximization

Gary Vaynerchuk's journey in personal branding showcases the remarkable power of a genuinely cultivated brand in boosting wealth. His journey to a multi-million dollar fortune is impressive, but the true worth of his efforts unfolds in the opportunities his brand unlocked. Early investments in giants like Facebook, Twitter, and Uber, along with building an invaluable personal network, underscore the real treasures behind his brand's success.

Gary Vee's story highlights the critical role of personal branding in our digital, interconnected era. It's more than just gaining recognition; it's about making your mark with something that truly matters. With a foundation built on authenticity, smart content creation, and genuine interaction, he provides a master plan for leveraging personal branding towards financial achievement. His journey reveals that effective personal branding goes beyond single projects, evolving into an endless wellspring of opportunities and expansion.

Chapter 6

The Investor's Mindset

"Patience is not simply the ability to wait - it's how we behave while we're waiting."

–Joyce Meyer

This quote resonated with me deeply the first time I read it, sparking a realization about the essential qualities of an investor's mindset: patience, resilience, and strategic foresight. Discovering the power of an investor's mindset was a turning point for me, much like unearthing a secret formula that could navigate the complex terrain of wealth maximization. It's fundamentally about how you think about investing. This realization has reshaped my financial journey, equipping me with the resilience to face the unpredictable waves of the market.

The essence of an investor's mindset lies in a blend of patience, discipline, emotional intelligence, and a visionary outlook. It's about transcending the daily market noise and focusing on your long-term financial horizon. Armed with a deep comprehension of your financial goals and risk tolerance, this mindset becomes your anchor, guiding your investment decisions and fueling your growth through continuous learning and adaptability.

Building Resilience through an Investor's Mindset

Embrace a Long-Term Vision

Think of the market's ups and downs as part of a longer narrative. During the 2008 financial crisis, those who kept their eyes on the horizon rather than the immediate turmoil saw their persistence pay off as markets rebounded. Their portfolios didn't just recover; they flourished.

Cultivate Emotional Intelligence

Being able to keep a cool head when the market heats up is invaluable. Emotional intelligence helps you make decisions based on sound analysis rather than getting caught in the grip of fear or greed. It's what keeps you from selling in a panic when the market dips or investing recklessly in a bubble about to burst.

Commit to Continuous Learning

The financial landscape is ever-evolving. During the COVID-19 pandemic, investors who swiftly adjusted their strategies to focus on booming sectors like technology and healthcare were able to mitigate losses and capitalize on new growth areas. Staying informed and adaptable is crucial.

Master Risk Management

Spread your investments to avoid putting all your eggs in one basket. Diversification across different asset classes and regions can safeguard your portfolio from significant losses. Employ strategies like stop-loss orders or hedging to manage your exposure to risk effectively.

Practice Discipline and Patience

Stick to your investment plan diligently and wait for the right opportunities. Avoid the temptation of market trends that don't align with your strategy. It's the disciplined waiting that often leads to the most significant gains, allowing the power of compounding to amplify your wealth.

An investor's mindset isn't something you're born with—it's cultivated through deliberate practice and a commitment to growth. By embracing these principles, you can fortify your journey toward wealth maximization. Navigate the market's inherent uncertainties not just with hope but with a strategy and a clear mind. Remember, managing your investments starts with managing your mindset. As you master your emotions and strategies, you'll find financial growth and a profound sense of confidence and control over your financial destiny.

Now, let's zoom in and explore how an investor's mindset deeply intertwines with long-term investment goals, particularly when navigating the often turbulent waters of market volatility. This journey isn't just about surviving the storms but thriving through them, by staying focused on the horizon.

Understanding Market Volatility

Market volatility is like the weather of the financial world—unpredictable, quick to change, and capable of turning sunny days into storms. These fluctuations are influenced by a myriad of factors, from economic data releases to geopolitical events. While these short-term waves can seem daunting, remember, they are a natural part of the investment landscape and often present opportunities for those with a long-term perspective.

The Importance of Long-Term Goals

Setting long-term investment goals is your anchor. It gives your strategy direction and helps you choose the right assets that align with your end-goals. More importantly, these goals act as a lighthouse, guiding you through the fog of market volatility. They help you maintain perspective and reduce the impulse to make hasty decisions that could veer you off course.

Strategies for Navigating Short-Term Volatility

Diversification: Think of your investment portfolio like a team, where each player has a unique role. Diversifying across different asset classes, sectors, and geographies means not all your eggs are in one basket. This strategy dilutes risk, ensuring that a hit in one area doesn't capsize your entire portfolio.

Dollar-Cost Averaging (DCA): This approach is about consistency. By investing a fixed amount regularly, you buy more when prices are low and less when they are high. Over time, this can lower the average cost per share, optimizing your investment returns without the need to time the market.

Rebalancing: Just as a gardener prunes a tree to maintain its health, periodically rebalancing your portfolio keeps it aligned with your goals. This might mean selling off assets that have done well and reinvesting in those that are lagging, thereby maintaining the balance you initially set.

Risk Management: Tools like stop-loss orders are like safety nets, minimizing potential falls. Knowing your risk tolerance helps you avoid making decisions that are too daring for your comfort, which is crucial during volatile times.

Emotional Discipline: Finally, the cornerstone of navigating market volatility is emotional discipline. Resist the urge to sell in a panic during downturns. Decisions made in haste are like leaving the safety of a shelter in a storm—risky and often unnecessary.

Remember, the key to thriving through market volatility lies in the steadfastness with which you adhere to your long-term goals. It's about managing your mindset as diligently as you manage your money. Stay disciplined, stay informed, and let your long-term objectives lead your way.

Treading through the COVID-19 crisis was a defining moment for many investors, including myself. Witnessing the sharp market declines and the subsequent recovery reinforced a crucial lesson: maintaining a disciplined, long-term investment approach during periods of volatility is potentially rewarding. Let's dive into how investors who either stayed the course during this crisis or strategically bought during dips benefited significantly over the long run.

Staying the Course

When the pandemic initially hit, the markets plunged dramatically, mirroring the global sense of uncertainty. The S&P 500, for instance, fell nearly 34% from its peak in February 2020 to its trough in March 2020. This kind of drop can test any investor's resolve. However, those who resisted the urge to sell during this downturn witnessed a robust recovery in the subsequent months. This resilience is reminiscent of past crises, such as the 1987 market crash, where markets recovered and continued to climb.

The lesson here is clear: the markets have a proven track record of recovery. Staying invested during these downturns allows you to benefit from the eventual upswings, underscoring the importance of looking beyond immediate fears towards a broader, more optimistic market horizon.

Buying During Dips

The COVID-19 market dip presented a unique opportunity for those with the liquidity and foresight to invest when prices were at their lowest. This strategy, known as 'buying the dip,' is based on the understanding that markets are cyclical, and downturns are often followed by recoveries. Those who invested during these lows were positioned for substantial gains as the market corrected itself.

Take, for instance, sectors like technology and healthcare during the pandemic. These sectors rebounded and thrived, driven by the surge in demand for digital and health-related services. Investors who targeted these sectors during the downturn benefited immensely as their values skyrocketed in the months that followed.

The pandemic also highlighted the critical role of diversification and risk management. Investors with diversified portfolios were better shielded from the brunt of the market's lows and could capitalize on the growth of sectors that were less impacted by, or even benefited from, the pandemic conditions. Diversification across various asset classes, sectors, and geographies is a tried-and-true strategy for mitigating risk and enhancing portfolio resilience during volatile times.

Finally, the COVID-19 crisis underscored the value of maintaining a long-term perspective. While the market's short-term gyrations can be disconcerting, they also open up opportunities to acquire valuable assets at a discount. However, it's crucial to acknowledge that timing the market perfectly is nearly impossible. Instead, focusing on solid fundamentals and a diversified, long-term strategy often yields the best results.

Warren Buffett, at the 2021 Berkshire Hathaway annual meeting, reiterated this view by advising investors to avoid trying to time the market. Instead, he recommended investing in a diversified portfolio of U.S. equities for the long term, highlighting the strength of a well-considered investment approach.

The COVID-19 crisis, much like other financial upheavals, has been both a test and a testament to the strength of maintaining discipline and a long-term view in investing. Those who stayed their course or seized the opportunity to buy during market lows have seen their resilience rewarded as markets recovered. This approach helps in riding out current storms and in preparing for future ones.

From my experience, one of the most crucial decisions in investing is knowing when to hold onto an investment, especially amidst the inevitable ebbs and flows of the market. Let's dive into the specific criteria that should guide this decision, focusing on the investment's fundamentals and how they align with your long-term goals.

Evaluating the Fundamentals of an Investment

Quality of the Business and Competitive Advantage

To judge whether to hold an investment, start by scrutinizing the quality of the business. This involves looking at the company's competitive edge, its position in the market, and the strength of its brand. A company that consistently outperforms its competitors usually has a durable "moat" that helps it sustain profitability even during tough times. If your investment is in a business that leads its field with innovation and customer loyalty, it's a strong candidate for holding, despite market fluctuations.

Financial Health and Stability

Next, assess the company's financial health. Important metrics to consider include the growth in revenue, profit margins, efficiency of cash flow, and the level of debt. A solid balance sheet and strong cash reserves are good indicators that the company can weather economic downturns and take advantage of growth opportunities when they arise. Stability in these areas often translates to less volatility in the stock's performance, making it a safer hold in the long term.

Management Quality

The caliber of a company's leadership is pivotal. A competent management team that can demonstrate strategic foresight and a clear execution plan is invaluable, especially in challenging times. Trust in the company's leadership to navigate through market cycles can be a decisive factor in holding onto an investment.

Growth Prospects and Innovation

Analyze the company's future growth potential. Companies that continuously innovate and adapt to changing market conditions are more likely to thrive. Look for investments in companies that are expanding into new markets or developing new products, as these activities can drive future returns.

Dividend Yield and Payout Stability

For those focused on income, the reliability and potential growth of dividends are crucial. A stable or increasing dividend yield, supported by strong earnings and cash flow, provides regular income and signals financial health. However, it's important to verify that these dividends aren't compromising the company's ability to invest in future growth.

Valuation Relative to Fundamentals

Finally, always compare the current valuation of the investment with its fundamental intrinsic value. If your analysis suggests that the stock is undervalued based on its earnings, cash flow, or asset value, it might be wise to maintain your position. On the other hand, an overvalued stock might require a reevaluation of its place in your portfolio.

Holding an investment requires a detailed analysis of the company's fundamentals and a clear understanding of how it fits within your broader financial strategy. Each of the points outlined above provides a lens through which you can assess the potential of your investments to withstand market turbulence and contribute to your long-term financial objectives.

The investment landscape has taught me that knowing when to exit is as critical as knowing when to enter. It's a decision that should be informed by a clear understanding of both the market and your personal investment strategy. Let's discuss the signals that might indicate it's time to sell an investment, ensuring these moves align with your long-term financial goals.

Recognizing the Signs to Sell

Deterioration in the Company's Fundamentals

When the core strengths of a business begin to wane—be it through loss of competitive advantage, deteriorating financial health, or both—it's crucial to reassess its place in your portfolio. For example, consider a company that was once a leader in its industry but has failed to keep pace with technological advancements, much like BlackBerry struggled against smartphones from Apple and Samsung. Similarly, a company facing mounting debts and shrinking profits, such as General Electric in recent years, may also signal a time to sell.

Changes in the Industry or Sector

External changes like new regulations or disruptive technologies can undermine a business's profitability. The tobacco industry, for instance, has been heavily impacted by regulatory changes, which might prompt a reassessment of investment in such companies. Likewise, the seismic shifts caused by streaming services have drastically altered the landscape for traditional media and entertainment businesses.

Misalignment with Investment Strategy

Your personal investment goals are pivotal in guiding your decisions. If your objectives or the time horizon for your investments shift—perhaps as retirement approaches—then it might be necessary to adjust your holdings to include more income-focused securities. Additionally, if a single stock or sector has grown to dominate your portfolio, reducing that concentration by selling some of your holdings could help manage risk and improve diversification.

Valuation Concerns

When a company's stock price far exceeds its intrinsic value based on fundamental analysis, the risk of a significant correction increases. For instance, Tesla's stock price surged in 2020 to levels that many analysts considered unsustainable relative to its earnings and revenue, prompting discussions about whether it was time to realize profits.

Better Opportunities Elsewhere

Sometimes, the decision to sell comes down to the potential for higher returns elsewhere. If an investment is underperforming and another opportunity presents a clearer advantage or aligns better with your growth expectations, reallocating your resources could enhance your overall portfolio performance.

Changes in Management or Strategy

Leadership changes can also be a trigger for selling. A new CEO with a questionable track record, or a company losing a visionary leader, can affect future growth prospects and investor confidence. Similarly, if a company pivots to a new business model that doesn't seem to fit its core strengths, it might be time to reconsider your investment.

Deciding to sell an investment involves more than reacting to the ups and downs of stock prices. It requires a thorough analysis of fundamental changes within the company, shifts in the external environment, and alignment with your personal investment strategy. By staying attuned to these factors and maintaining a disciplined approach, you can make informed decisions that safeguard your investments and optimize your financial outcomes. This proactive approach allows you to control your investment journey, making adjustments as necessary to achieve your long-term financial objectives.

As I reflect on the journey of diversifying my investment portfolio, I recognize that stepping beyond the conventional domain of stocks and bonds has pened up new avenues for growth aimed at wealth maximisation. This evolution in my investment strategy was driven by a desire to explore territories that could cushion against market downturns and amplify potential returns. Here's a closer look at how branching into alternative investments, embracing geographic diversification, and implementing sector-specific strategies can enhance and protect your portfolio.

Alternative Investments

Real Estate: Including real estate in your portfolio can provide a dual benefit of income generation through rental yields and potential capital gains. Whether directly purchasing property or investing indirectly through Real Estate Investment Trusts (REITs), real estate offers a tangible asset that often exhibits less correlation with stock market fluctuations, thus providing a stabilizing effect during periods of volatility.

Private Equity and Venture Capital: Engaging in private equity or venture capital involves investing in private companies, from startups to well-established entities. This avenue can be lucrative, offering substantial returns if these companies succeed and go public or are sold at a premium. The high-risk and long-term nature of these investments require a strategic approach and a tolerance for potential initial losses in anticipation of significant later gains.

Commodities: Adding commodities like gold, oil, and agricultural products to your portfolio can serve as an effective hedge against inflation and currency fluctuations. Gold, especially, is often considered a safe haven in times of economic instability. The key benefit of including commodities is their low correlation with stocks and bonds, which can reduce overall portfolio volatility.

Hedge Funds: Hedge funds use diverse strategies to achieve returns in various market conditions, employing tactics such as leverage, short selling, and derivatives trading. Although potentially offering high returns and diversification, hedge funds often come with higher fees and are generally available only to accredited investors.

Geographic Diversification

Emerging Markets: Venturing into emerging markets can significantly enhance growth potential. Nations like China, India, and Brazil present opportunities due to their large consumer bases and rapid technological and economic advancements. However, it's crucial to consider the associated risks, including political instability and currency volatility.

Developed Markets: Incorporating equities and bonds from developed markets outside your home country helps mitigate country-specific risks. Investing in regions like Europe or Japan can diversify your exposure and tap into established industries and companies that lead globally in areas such as pharmaceuticals, automotive, and technology.

Expanding your portfolio beyond traditional stocks and bonds to include alternative investments and geographic diversification is about strategically positioning yourself to capture growth from a variety of sources. Each investment type and market brings its characteristics and potential benefits to the table, making it imperative to understand their roles within your broader investment strategy. By thoughtfully integrating these elements, you can build a resilient, well-rounded portfolio poised for long-term success. Remember, the goal is to align these investment choices with your overall financial objectives, ensuring that each move is a step toward achieving your ultimate financial ambitions.

Reflecting on the stories of successful companies like Apple can profoundly illuminate the paths we might take toward wealth maximization. Delving into Apple's history, we see a narrative brimming with the resilience and foresight of its early investors. These investors, who weathered significant challenges and embraced pivotal opportunities, offer us a template for employing an investor's mindset that is both dynamic and disciplined.

Apple's Early Days

Initial Investment and Vision: Back in 1977, Apple's promise lay in its innovative approach to personal computing, which caught the eye of investors like Mike Markkula. His $250,000 investment was a substantial bet on Apple's potential to redefine the tech landscape. This wasn't merely financial support; it was a profound belief in Apple's vision, which was crucial during the company's formative years.

Staying the Course Through Challenges: Apple's journey wasn't smooth, marred by leadership battles and competitive pressures, notably Steve Jobs' ousting in 1985. Yet, those who saw these hurdles as temporary could stay invested, focusing on the company's core value and potential for innovation.

The Importance of Strategic Decisions

Recognizing Transformational Products: The launches of the iPod in 2001 and the iPhone in 2007 were game changers not just for Apple but for technology as a whole. Investors who understood the impact these products could have were positioned to reap substantial rewards as Apple's valuation skyrocketed.

Adapting to Market Changes: Apple's strategic pivot towards a services-oriented business model in response to slowing hardware sales represents a critical lesson in adaptability. For investors, recognizing and supporting this shift was key to capitalizing on Apple's continued growth in the face of evolving market dynamics.

Lessons for Wealth Maximization

Long-Term Vision: The foresight to see beyond immediate challenges and recognize long-term potential was instrumental. Those who maintained their investment in Apple from its nascent stages through its rise to a trillion-dollar entity exemplify the power of a long-term investment perspective.

Understanding the Business: Comprehensive knowledge of Apple's operations, competitive edge, and industry position enabled early investors to make well-informed decisions. This deep understanding is crucial to identifying companies that have robust growth prospects.

Risk Tolerance and Conviction: Early investments in transformative companies like Apple require not only capital but also the courage to back unproven ideas. The success of such investments hinges on an investor's conviction in the company's leadership and vision, balanced by a willingness to embrace risk.

Adaptability: Successful investors recognize and adapt to strategic shifts within their investment targets. Apple's evolution underscores the importance of being flexible and responsive to new strategies and market conditions.

Diversification: While Apple's success is compelling, it also highlights the risks of over-concentration in a single investment. A diversified portfolio remains a cornerstone of risk management and wealth maximization, ensuring that the impact of any single investment's failure is mitigated.

The journey of early Apple investors teaches us that successful investing demands vision, patience, and an unwavering commitment to understanding and adapting to the market's ebbs and flows. These lessons underscore the essence of a sophisticated investor's mindset—focused yet flexible, informed yet intuitive—equipping us with the strategies to navigate the complexities of investing in a dynamic market landscape.

Reflecting on the tales of early adopters in the investment world reveals an exhilarating path of high stakes and even higher rewards. It's a path I've traversed through my own investing journey, particularly in emerging markets and innovative sectors where the fusion of risk and opportunity shapes a landscape ripe for substantial gains.

Early Adopters in Emerging Markets

China's E-Commerce Boom: Consider the story of Alibaba, which at its IPO in 2014, not only shattered records by raising

$25 billion but also heralded the immense potential of China's consumer market. Investors who entered early into Alibaba's narrative did so by recognizing the disruptive force of its business model in a booming market. Despite the inherent risks of a new and fluctuating market, these investors saw their foresight richly rewarded as they capitalized on Alibaba's meteoric rise.

India's Market Growth: Similarly, the Indian market has proven fertile ground for those with the patience to endure its volatility. Investors who committed to the Indian market, driven by the country's significant demographic and economic potentials—such as a young population and a growing digital infrastructure—have experienced considerable returns. These investors navigated through political turbulence and regulatory unpredictability, armed with a robust strategy that aligned with the country's growth trajectory.

Lessons for Wealth Maximization

Conduct Thorough Research: In high-risk markets, success often begins with rigorous research. Understanding the nuances of the market's political, economic, and regulatory climates is crucial and can help mitigate potential risks.

Diversification: To manage the inherent risks, diversification is key. Spreading investments across various emerging markets and sectors can safeguard against the volatility and uncertainty that any single market might present.

Long-Term Perspective: Embracing a long-term perspective is essential, especially in markets characterized by rapid but uneven growth. While short-term fluctuations can be disconcerting, the broader upward trajectory of emerging economies can offer rewarding returns for those who are patient.

Risk Tolerance: A high tolerance for risk is indispensable for early adopters. The potential for substantial gains in high-risk investments often comes hand-in-hand with the possibility of significant fluctuations and even losses.

Leverage Expertise: Engaging with financial advisors or tapping into the expertise of seasoned investment firms can provide crucial guidance and risk management strategies, enhancing the chances of success in complex investment landscapes.

Stay Informed: Keeping up-to-date with global economic trends and market shifts is vital. The investment landscape is dynamic, and being informed can help you adjust your strategies in response to new developments.

Embrace Innovation: Finally, recognizing and investing in innovation can lead to considerable advantages. Early adopters often invest in companies at the cutting edge of new technologies or business models, positioning themselves to benefit from these companies' growth and industry impact.

The experiences of early adopters in markets like China and India offer powerful insights into navigating high-risk, high-reward investment environments. These stories underscore the importance of a calculated, informed approach to investing—one that balances the excitement of potential gains with the prudence of strategic risk management.

Navigating the rollercoaster of the market requires a mix of resilience to weather volatility, the savvy to know when to stick or twist, and the vision to grab onto diversification and fresh opportunities. That's the secret recipe for a solid investment strategy.

Diving into the stories of early adopters and investment pros, we uncover a golden nugget of wisdom: every investment has its own tale of risk and reward. By adopting a disciplined, well-informed, and proactive stance in our investment game, we're setting ourselves up to flourish, transforming potential upheavals into golden opportunities for remarkable growth.

Let's keep pushing towards financial mastery, adapting our strategies to match the ever-changing markets and our personal life goals. By embracing continuous learning, keeping an eye on the long-term prize, and learning from our wins and losses, we'll make our investment journey enlightening and incredibly rewarding too.

Chapter 7

A Nuanced Guide to the Tax Landscape

"Nothing is certain except death and taxes."

You've probably heard this saying before. It's often used to highlight the inevitability of taxes in our lives.

When we talk about taxes, it can feel like there's a lot to figure out. Some of us are new to this, while others have been doing it for years, yet the complexity seems to remain constant. In this chapter, we'll explore the basics of income tax slabs and take a closer look at the exemptions and deductions you can use to save on taxes. I'll walk you through a guide on how you can make the most out of the current tax laws.

If you're someone who's just started working, an entrepreneur managing your own business, or a retiree with unique tax considerations, I'll cover what you need to know.

Understanding Income Tax Slabs and Benefits

Income tax in India follows a tiered structure, where your tax rate depends on your income level and age group. This section will cover the current income tax slabs for the financial year 2023-24 and assessment year 2024-25.

The rates increase progressively as your income rises, so higher earners pay a higher percentage of their income in taxes. Let's break down what these numbers mean.

For individuals under 60 years of age, the income tax slabs are as follows:

Up to Rs 3,00,000:	No tax
Rs 3,00,000 to Rs 6,00,000:	5% on the income exceeding Rs 3,00,000
Rs 6,00,000 to Rs 9,00,000:	10% on the income exceeding Rs 6,00,000
Rs 9,00,000 to Rs 12,00,000:	15% on the income exceeding Rs 9,00,000
Rs 12,00,000 to Rs 15,00,000:	20% on the income exceeding Rs 12,00,000
Above Rs 15,00,000:	30%

For senior citizens between 60 and 80 years, the tax slabs are:

Up to Rs 3,00,000:	No tax
Rs 3,00,000 to Rs 5,00,000:	5% on the income exceeding Rs 3,00,000
Rs 5,00,000 to Rs 10,00,000:	20%
Above Rs 10,00,000:	30%.

For super senior citizens above 80 years, the slabs are a bit different:

Up to Rs 5,00,000:	No tax
Rs 5,00,000 to Rs 10,00,000:	20%
Above Rs 10,00,000:	30%.

Special considerations for senior citizens include an increased exemption limit, acknowledging their unique financial situations. These rates are part of the old tax regime, which offers more deductions and exemptions.

The new tax regime simplifies the structure but offers fewer deductions. Its slabs are:

Up to Rs 3,00,000:	No tax
Rs 3,00,000 to Rs 6,00,000:	5% on the income exceeding Rs 3,00,000
Rs 6,00,000 to Rs 9,00,000:	10% on the income exceeding Rs 6,00,000
Rs 9,00,000 to Rs 12,00,000:	15% on the income exceeding Rs 9,00,000
Rs 12,00,000 to Rs 15,00,000:	20%
Above Rs 15,00,000:	30%.

The choice between the new and old tax regimes depends on your financial situation, whether you benefit from more deductions, and your investment strategy.

Let's explore some common exemptions and deductions, such as those found in Section 80C, 80D, and others, along with tax reliefs for home loans, education loans, and more.

Tax Benefits Under Section 80C

Section 80C is a popular section that offers various tax-saving opportunities. You can claim a deduction of up to Rs 1,50,000 each financial year for certain types of investments and expenditures. This deduction can significantly reduce your taxable income, leading to lower tax liability. Here are some common ways to make the most of Section 80C:

- Life Insurance Premiums: Premiums paid for life insurance policies can be deducted.
- Public Provident Fund (PPF): Contributions to PPF accounts are tax-deductible.
- Equity-Linked Saving Schemes (ELSS): Investments in ELSS mutual funds are eligible for deduction under Section 80C.
- Home Loan Principal: If you have a home loan, the principal repayment is deductible under this section.
- National Savings Certificate (NSC) and other similar instruments .

– **Health Insurance Benefits Under Section 80D**

Section 80D provides deductions for health insurance premiums paid for self, family, and parents. The deduction limit is Rs 25,000 for individuals and Rs 50,000 for senior citizens. This section also covers preventive health check-ups, allowing you to claim a deduction of up to Rs 5,000 within the overall limit.

– **Tax Deductions for Home Loans**

Apart from the principal repayment under Section 80C, you can also claim a deduction for the interest paid on home loans. Section 24(b) allows you to deduct up to Rs 2,00,000 for self-occupied property. For rental properties, the entire interest paid is deductible, subject to certain limits and conditions.

- **Education Loan Benefits**

  Section 80E provides a deduction for the interest paid on education loans. This can be for your education or for a family member's. The deduction is available for up to 8 years from the start of loan repayment, with no upper limit on the amount you can claim.

Investing in ELSS Funds

ELSS funds are a type of mutual fund that primarily invest in equities. They offer tax benefits under Section 80C, allowing you to claim deductions of up to Rs 1,50,000 in a financial year, which can significantly reduce your taxable income. One of the key features of ELSS is its lock-in period of three years—the shortest among tax-saving instruments. This means your investment cannot be withdrawn for three years, promoting long-term investing

The equity component in ELSS funds offers the potential for higher returns compared to other tax-saving instruments like Public Provident Fund (PPF) and National Savings Certificate (NSC). Because ELSS funds invest in equities, they carry more risk, but they also have a higher chance of delivering significant returns over time.

Another advantage is that ELSS allows for Systematic Investment Plans (SIPs). This means you can invest a fixed amount regularly, which can help you benefit from rupee cost averaging and compound interest over the years. It's a flexible and accessible way to participate in the stock market while enjoying tax benefits

When comparing ELSS to other tax-saving instruments, such as PPF and NSC, there are a few points to consider:

- **Lock-in Period:** ELSS has a lock-in period of three years, which is shorter than PPF's 15 years and NSC's 5 years.
- **Returns:** The equity-based nature of ELSS can lead to higher returns, but it also carries more risk. PPF and NSC provide guaranteed returns, albeit at lower rates.
- **Tax Benefits:** All these instruments offer tax benefits under Section 80C, but ELSS has a higher potential for growth due to its equity component.

Understanding these differences can help you decide which investment vehicle aligns with your financial goals and risk appetite. ELSS can be an attractive option if you're comfortable with a bit more risk and are looking for tax-saving opportunities that can also grow your wealth over time.

Public Provident Fund (PPF)

PPF is a long-term investment scheme backed by the government, known for its safety and stable returns. Here's what you need to know about PPF:

- **Lock-in Period:** PPF has a 15-year lock-in period. After this period, you can choose to extend it in blocks of five years or withdraw the full amount.

- **Interest Rate:** The interest rate is set by the government and is generally higher than standard savings accounts, making PPF a reliable option for steady growth.
- **Investment Limits:** You can invest a minimum of Rs 500 and a maximum of Rs 1,50,000 annually. Contributions can be made in lump sums or instalments.
- **Tax Benefits:** PPF investments are eligible for deduction under Section 80C, and the interest earned is tax-free. Additionally, the maturity amount is also exempt from tax

National Savings Certificate (NSC)

NSC is another government-backed investment scheme, providing a secure way to save with guaranteed returns. Here's what you should know about NSC:

- **Lock-in Period:** NSC has a 5-year lock-in period. Once this period ends, the certificate matures, and you can withdraw the total amount.
- **Interest Rate:** The interest rate for NSC is fixed at the time of purchase, ensuring consistent returns over the 5-year period.
- **Investment Limits:** There's no maximum limit for NSC investment, but contributions are typically in denominations like Rs 100, Rs 500, Rs 1,000, Rs 5,000, and Rs 10,000.
- **Tax Benefits:** Like PPF, NSC offers tax benefits under Section 80C, allowing you to claim a deduction for your investments. However, unlike PPF, the interest earned

on NSC is taxable, even though it is reinvested into the scheme during the lock-in period

Comparison Between PPF and NSC

- **Lock-in Period:** PPF has a longer lock-in period of 15 years, while NSC has a shorter lock-in of 5 years.
- **Interest Rate:** PPF offers a variable rate set by the government, while NSC has a fixed rate at the time of purchase.
- **Tax Benefits:** Both PPF and NSC qualify for Section 80C, but PPF has tax-free interest and maturity, whereas NSC's interest is taxable.

Considering these factors, your choice between PPF and NSC depends on your investment goals, risk appetite, and preferred lock-in period. If you seek a stable, long-term investment with tax-free returns, PPF is an excellent choice. If you prefer a shorter commitment with guaranteed returns, NSC might be a better option

Insurance Products for Tax Saving

Insurance products can be an effective way to save on taxes while providing coverage for life risks. In this section, we explore term life insurance, Unit Linked Insurance Plans (ULIPs), and health insurance policies to understand their tax benefits and offer tips on choosing the right policy.

Insurance plays a crucial role in financial planning, and it can also be a valuable tool for tax-saving. Let's break down each type of insurance product and their tax benefits:

Term Life Insurance

Term life insurance provides pure life coverage for a specific period. If the policyholder dies within the term, the beneficiary receives the sum assured. Since it doesn't have an investment component, term life insurance is often more affordable than other life insurance policies.

Tax Benefits

- Premiums paid for term life insurance are deductible under Section 80C, up to Rs 1,50,000 per year.
- The death benefit received by the nominee is exempt from tax under Section 10(10D), making it a tax-efficient way to provide financial security to your family (indiafilings).

Unit Linked Insurance Plans (ULIPs)

ULIPs combine life insurance with investment. A portion of the premium goes towards life coverage, while the rest is invested in equity, debt, or hybrid funds, allowing for potential growth over time.

Tax Benefits

- Premiums paid for ULIPs are also deductible under Section 80C, up to Rs 1,50,000 per year.
- The returns on maturity are exempt from tax if the premium paid does not exceed 10% of the sum assured. This makes ULIPs an attractive option for those seeking insurance with an investment component.

Health Insurance Policies

Health insurance policies cover medical expenses for policyholders and their families. Having health insurance is not only crucial for healthcare coverage but also provides tax benefits.

Tax Benefits

- Premiums paid for health insurance are deductible under Section 80D, up to Rs 25,000 for individuals and Rs 50,000 for senior citizens.
- This deduction applies to policies covering yourself, your spouse, children, and parents.
- Preventive health check-ups are also included under Section 80D, with a deduction limit of Rs 5,000.

Tips on Choosing the Right Policy

When choosing an insurance policy for tax-saving, consider the following tips:

- **Assess Your Needs:** Determine whether you need life insurance, health insurance, or both. Your age, financial dependents, and health status are key factors.
- **Understand the Tax Benefits:** Familiarize yourself with the tax advantages each policy offers. This will help you make an informed decision.
- **Compare Policies:** Look at different insurance providers and their offerings. Consider factors like coverage, premiums, and additional benefits.

- **Check Flexibility and Transparency:** Ensure the policy you choose offers flexibility in terms of premium payment, sum assured, and maturity benefits. Transparency in terms of charges and fees is also crucial.

By considering these factors, you can select an insurance policy that not only provides the coverage you need but also helps you save on taxes.

Strategic tax planning can make a huge difference when it comes to reducing your tax liability. If you're looking to lower your taxes, here's a personal tip: consider using tax-loss harvesting to offset capital gains. This strategy can help you manage your capital gains taxes by selling off losing investments, turning those losses into a way to balance out your gains.

Here's how I would approach tax-loss harvesting:

- **Look at Your Investments:** Take some time to review your portfolio and identify securities that have lost value. These are your potential candidates for tax-loss harvesting. It's not always easy to sell at a loss, but this is about reducing your tax bill.

- **Find Your Capital Gains:** Figure out where you have realized capital gains. This could be from selling stocks, real estate, or even a business. If you have gains, you can offset them with your losses.

- **Sell the Losers:** Once you've identified the investments with losses, you might consider selling them to realize the loss. This loss can offset your gains, lowering your taxable income. For example, if you have Rs 1,00,000 in capital gains and Rs 50,000 in realized losses, you only owe taxes on the Rs 50,000 difference.

- **Avoid Wash-Sale Rules:** When you sell at a loss, be careful not to trigger wash-sale rules, which happen if you buy back a substantially identical security within 30 days before or after the sale. This can disallow the tax benefit, which isn't ideal if you're trying to minimize your tax burden.

- **Claim the Losses on Your Tax Return:** When you file your tax return, make sure to report your realized capital losses to offset the gains. If your losses exceed your gains, the good news is that you can carry them forward to future years, using them to offset future capital gains

Let's say you made a capital gain of Rs 2,00,000 from selling some shares. If you also have Rs 1,50,000 in losses from other stocks, selling those can offset your gains, leaving you with a taxable gain of Rs 50,000 instead of Rs 2,00,000. That's a huge difference when you're looking at taxes.

Using tax-loss harvesting can be a smart move, but you have to be strategic about it. If you're unsure, it's worth talking to a tax advisor or a financial planner to ensure you're following the rules and maximizing your tax benefits

When it comes to taxes, holding periods matter. Understanding the tax implications of holding various asset classes—stocks, bonds, and real estate—is crucial for strategic tax planning. Let me break it down for you, giving you the key insights to help you make informed decisions.

Tax Implications of Holding Periods for Various Asset Classes

Different asset classes have varying tax treatments based on how long you hold them. Here's what you need to know about the tax implications for some common asset classes:

Stocks

Stocks have different tax rates depending on the holding period:

- **Short-term Capital Gains (STCG):** If you sell stocks within 12 months of buying them, the gains are taxed at a flat rate of 15%.
- **Long-term Capital Gains (LTCG):** If you hold stocks for more than 12 months before selling, the gains are taxed at 10%, but only if the gains exceed Rs 1,00,000. Anything below that is exempt.

Bonds

Bonds can also be categorized by holding periods:

- **Short-term Capital Gains:** If you sell bonds within 36 months, the gains are added to your income and taxed at the applicable slab rate.
- **Long-term Capital Gains:** If you hold bonds for more than 36 months, the gains are taxed at 20% with indexation benefits, which adjust the gains for inflation.

Real Estate

Real estate has longer holding periods and distinct tax implications:

- **Short-term Capital Gains:** If you sell real estate within 24 months, the gains are added to your income and taxed at your normal slab rate.
- **Long-term Capital Gains:** If you hold real estate for more than 24 months, the gains are taxed at 20% with indexation benefits

Strategic Tips for Holding Periods

- **Plan Your Investments:** Consider the holding periods for various asset classes before investing. If you plan to sell within a shorter timeframe, understand the higher tax rates that apply.
- **Use Indexation for Long-term Investments:** Indexation benefits can help you reduce the tax burden on long-term capital gains. By adjusting for inflation, you can lower the taxable gains and pay less in taxes.
- **Consider Tax-advantaged Accounts:** Some investments, like those in Public Provident Fund (PPF), have longer holding periods but offer tax advantages at maturity and during the investment phase.

When planning your tax strategy, consider your investment goals and holding periods for different assets. Whether you're dealing with stocks, bonds, or real estate, understanding the tax implications can help you make better financial decisions and minimize your tax burden. If you're unsure about specific cases, consulting with a financial advisor or tax professional is always a good idea.

Chapter 8

Mastering The Indian Stock Market

As dawn breaks over the Dikhu River in Nagaland, members of the Ao and Sumi tribes prepare for a day of fishing. They are guided by centuries-old wisdom, understanding the river's currents and rhythms to skillfully catch fish. These fishermen use traditional, simple tools, reflecting their deep connection with the river and its cycles.

In the world of investing, especially in the fast-moving Indian stock market, there's a similarity with fishing. Just like how these fishermen know when to cast their nets for the best catch, investors need to know the best times to buy or sell stocks. Understanding the market's trends is key to success, just as knowing the river currents is for fishermen. Our look at the Indian stock market will be strategic and patient, guided by a deep understanding of the market.

Analysis of Current and Emerging High-Growth Sectors in the Indian Economy

The Indian economy,is teeming with sectors brimming with potential for promising growth. Recent trends and economic indicators have identified several sectors not just primed for vigorous expansion but also set to make a substantial impact on the wider economic landscape.

Manufacturing Renaissance

One of the standout performers in the current economic climate is the manufacturing sector. With a robust year-on-year growth rate of 11.6%, this sector benefits from both government incentives and increasing domestic and international demand. Initiatives like "Make in India" have bolstered manufacturing, turning it into a cornerstone for investors looking for sustainable growth.Companies such as Tata Motors and Mahindra have expanded their manufacturing capabilities, capitalizing on policy support to boost production.The sector's surge is not just a reflection of temporary demand but a result of structural changes that promise long-term benefits.

Construction and Infrastructure Boom

Parallel to manufacturing, the construction sector is experiencing a significant upswing, driven by massive public and private investments in infrastructure. With a growth rate of 9.5%, the sector is riding the wave of increased capital expenditure by the government, aimed at enhancing the country's infrastructure. Major projects like the Delhi-Mumbai Industrial Corridor aim to develop new industrial cities as "Smart Cities" and upgrade the infrastructure, creating vast opportunities for companies like Larsen & Toubro and DLF.The focus on building smart cities and improving transportation networks has opened a plethora of investment opportunities within this sector.

Services Sector

While the services sector has seen a slight deceleration, it continues to be a major growth driver, contributing significantly to the GDP. Firms like Infosys and TCS stand at the forefront, driving growth through digital transformation projects across global markets. This sector's resilience is underpinned by sustained demand for IT solutions and services

These IT and software services, in particular, remain strong, buoyed by the global digital transformation wave. This sector's resilience and innovation-driven growth make it a safe harbor for investors seeking stability amidst the dynamic economic currents.

Emerging Sectors: FMCG and E-commerce

The Fast-Moving Consumer Goods (FMCG) sector, along with e-commerce, is rapidly emerging as a growth leader. The shift towards online shopping and digital consumption has accelerated growth in these areas.ompanies like Hindustan Unilever and Flipkart are capitalizing on these trends, driven by increased consumer spending and supportive government policies.The government's supportive policies, coupled with a rising middle class's increased spending power, have made these sectors attractive for long-term investments.

Spotting these opportunities lets investors position their portfolios to gain from India's economic growth. Like fishermen on the Dikhu River observing the currents, investors can skillfully navigate the market's complexities with informed precision.

Let's now discuss what is considered the cornerstone of smart investing: Index Fund Investing. This method offers a strategic way to participate in these high-growth sectors without the need to pick individual stocks, simplifying investment decisions and potentially reducing risks.

Index Fund Investing

Index funds have become a staple in the portfolio of the modern investor, offering a way to gain exposure to a broad market or specific sectors with a single investment. These funds track a market index, such as the NIFTY 50 or SENSEX, and are designed to mirror the performance of these indices. By investing in an index fund, you inherently diversify your holdings, spreading out potential risks across a wide array of stocks rather than depending on the success of a few.

This method of investing has garnered wide appreciation for its ability to provide investors with a passive, yet effective means of participating in the financial markets.

Simplicity and Cost Efficiency

One of the key advantages of index funds is their simplicity. These funds aim to replicate the performance of a specific index, such as the S&P BSE Sensex or the Nifty 50, which are barometers for the Indian markets. By investing in an index fund, you are essentially buying a portfolio that mirrors the composition and performance of these indexes without the need to analyze individual stocks.

Furthermore, index funds are known for their lower cost. Unlike actively managed funds, where fund managers constantly buy and sell assets to outperform the market, index funds follow a passive investment strategy. This means they incur fewer transaction fees and management costs, which can significantly erode investment returns over time. Studies and financial analyses consistently show that lower expense ratios can lead to higher net returns for investors, especially in a market as diverse and dynamic as India's.

Let's consider the UTI Nifty Index Fund, which has one of the lower expense ratios in the category, typically around 0.2%. This is substantially lower than the average actively managed fund, which might charge between 1% to 2.5%. The lower expense ratio translates directly into higher returns for investors, particularly noticeable over long investment horizons.

Comparison with Actively Managed Funds

While actively managed funds can and do outperform the market in certain instances, they often come with higher fees that can offset potential gains. Active management involves greater research and transaction costs as fund managers attempt to leverage market inefficiencies and timing strategies to surpass the performance of a benchmark index.

However, data and market studies, including those from major market analysts and financial institutions, often highlight that actively managed funds do not consistently outperform index funds over the long term. The consistency and predictability of index funds make them an attractive option for investors who prefer a more hands-off approach to investing.

Actively managed funds, like the HDFC Top 100 Fund, aim to outperform stock market indices by selecting stocks that fund managers believe will perform better than others. While this fund has had periods of outperformance relative to the broader market, it also charges a higher expense ratio, which can erode some of the excess returns.

Statistically, over long periods, many actively managed funds struggle to consistently beat their benchmark indices after accounting for fees. For instance, during a 10-year period, the S&P BSE 200 Index might outperform 60-80% of actively managed large-cap funds in India, highlighting the challenge and added cost of trying to beat the market through active management.

Selecting the Best Index Fund

When choosing an index fund, investors should consider several factors to align their investment with their financial goals. These include the fund's tracking error, which measures how closely a fund follows its index. A lower tracking error indicates a fund that more accurately replicates the index's performance. Additionally, the expense ratio is crucial—lower costs generally lead to better net returns.

Investors should also evaluate the liquidity of the fund. Funds with higher average daily trading volumes are generally easier to buy and sell without affecting the price too much. This is particularly important in volatile markets where the ability to enter or exit positions quickly can be crucial.

When selecting an index fund, factors such as tracking error and expense ratio are paramount. The SBI Nifty Index Fund is known for its low tracking error relative to the Nifty 50 Index, indicating its effectiveness in replicating the performance of the index it tracks.

For liquidity, funds like the ICICI Prudential Nifty Index Fund are notable. This fund trades with high volume, ensuring that investors can easily enter and exit positions without significant price impacts. This is particularly advantageous during periods of high market volatility when quick moves can help preserve capital or capture gains.

Index funds offer a robust foundation for building a diversified investment portfolio, especially suited to the evolving dynamics of the Indian stock market. They provide a practical solution for investors looking to benefit from the growth of the overall market or specific sectors within it, without the complexities and higher costs associated with active management.

Derivatives Trading

Derivatives trading, specifically through instruments such as futures and options, represents a sophisticated area of finance that leverages the future values of assets. These tools are not just financial agreements but strategic devices that investors and traders use to hedge against potential losses or to speculate for potential gains.

Understanding Futures

Futures contracts are agreements to buy or sell an asset at a predetermined price at a specified time in the future. These are standardized in terms of quality, quantity, and delivery time, traded on exchanges like the National Stock Exchange (NSE) and the Bombay Stock Exchange (BSE) in India. For example, an investor might use a futures contract to lock in the price of a stock or commodity, thereby hedging against the risk of price fluctuations. This is particularly useful in sectors like agriculture, where price volatility is frequent.

Futures are marked to market daily, meaning the changes in their market value are settled at the end of each trading day.

This feature requires participants to maintain a margin account, where funds must be deposited to cover potential losses, a critical aspect of futures trading that helps manage the high leverage typically associated with these instruments.

Consider a wheat farmer who is concerned about potential price drops by the time of harvest. To hedge against this risk, the farmer can enter into a futures contract to sell their wheat at a predetermined price on a set future date. For instance, assuming the current price is ₹2,000 per quintal, the farmer could lock in this price for their harvest due in six months. This contract obligates the farmer to deliver a specified amount of wheat at ₹2,000 per quintal, regardless of the market price at the time of delivery. If market prices fall to ₹1,500 per quintal at harvest, the farmer still receives ₹2,000 per quintal, effectively protecting their income against price volatility. This example shows how futures are used in commodity markets to stabilize revenues for producers.

Exploring Options

Options trading offers another layer of complexity and flexibility. An option gives the buyer the right, but not the obligation, to buy (call option) or sell (put option) an underlying asset at a specified strike price on or before a certain date. This right comes with a cost, known as a premium, which the buyer pays to the seller of the option.

Options can be used for hedging purposes, such as protecting a stock portfolio from a decline in market value by purchasing put options. For example, if you own shares of a company and fear the price might drop, buying a put option at a current price can help mitigate potential losses by allowing you to sell the shares at the strike price, regardless of how low the market price drops.

They can also be used for speculative purposes, where traders look to profit from their views on the direction of the market or a specific stock. The advantage here is the asymmetry in payoffs; the maximum loss for the buyer of an option is the premium paid, while the potential profit can be significant if the market moves favorably.

Imagine an investor who holds a significant amount of shares in a tech company and is worried about a potential downturn in the tech sector over the next three months. To protect their investment, the investor could buy put options for the stocks they own at a strike price close to the current market price. Let's say the stock is currently trading at ₹500 per share. The investor could buy a put option with a strike price of ₹500 expiring in three months for a premium of ₹30 per share.

If the stock price falls to ₹400, the investor can exercise the put option and sell the shares at the strike price of ₹500, thus minimizing their losses. The cost of this protection is the premium paid (₹30 per share), which is the maximum loss if the stock price remains stable or increases—thus the investor would not exercise the option. This scenario illustrates how options can serve as insurance against adverse movements in stock prices, allowing investors to manage potential risks while maintaining their positions in the market.

Terminology and Key Concepts

Understanding the terminology is crucial in derivatives trading. Key terms include:

- **Strike Price:** The price at which the underlying asset can be bought or sold if the option is exercised.
- **Expiration Date:** The date on which the option or future expires and ceases to exist.
- **Premium:** The price paid by the buyer of an option to the seller.
- **Underlying Asset:** The financial instrument on which the derivative is based, which can be stocks, bonds, commodities, currencies, interest rates, or market indexes.

Strategies for Using Derivatives for Hedging Risk and Speculative Trading

Derivatives trading offers two primary applications: hedging risk to protect investments and speculative trading to seek profit from market movements. Understanding how to leverage these strategies can significantly enhance an investor's portfolio management effectiveness.

Hedging Risk with Derivatives

Hedging is a way to protect against possible investment losses. For example, if a portfolio manager has a big investment in the car industry, which could lose value due to economic problems or changes in what customers want, they might use index options to safeguard their investment. Essentially, if they're worried about the market going down, they can buy put options on a car industry index. This acts like insurance. So, if the index falls, the money made from the put options can make up for any losses in the portfolio.

Imagine a jewelry manufacturer who requires a consistent supply of silver over the next year. Concerned about potential price increases in silver, which could significantly impact production costs, the manufacturer decides to hedge this risk using silver futures contracts. By purchasing futures contracts at a current price of ₹50,000 per kilogram, the manufacturer locks in this price for the duration of the contracts, thereby securing a stable cost basis despite potential future price volatility. If the market price of silver rises to ₹55,000 per kilogram in the following months, the futures contracts will offset the increased costs of purchasing silver at market prices.

This strategy is particularly useful for institutional investors who need to manage risks across diverse and extensive portfolios. It helps ensure stability and can protect the capital from unexpected market downturns, thereby securing long-term investment goals.

Speculative Trading for Profit

On the flip side, derivatives are powerful tools for speculative trading, where traders seek to profit from predicting market movements. For example, a trader might speculate that a particular stock will increase in price due to an upcoming product launch or favorable market conditions. By purchasing call options for that stock, the trader can potentially enjoy significant gains if the stock price rises as expected.

Consider a trader who anticipates that the shares of a leading tech company will rise due to upcoming product launches and positive market rumors. The trader buys call options on the stock with a strike price of ₹1,000, paying a premium of ₹50 per share. If the stock's market price climbs to ₹1,200, the trader can exercise the call options to buy shares at ₹1,000, selling them immediately at the market price of ₹1,200. This speculative move nets a profit of ₹150 per share (after accounting for the ₹50 premium), showcasing how options can leverage market predictions into substantial gains.

Speculative trading involves a higher risk as it relies on accurate market predictions and timing. However, the advantage of using options in speculative trading lies in their leverage effect—investors can control a large amount of stock for a relatively small cost (the premium paid for the options), which can result in high returns on investment if the market moves favorably.

Combining Hedging and Speculation

Astute investors often blend these strategies to balance their portfolios. For example, an investor might predominantly hedge to protect their core investments but allocate a smaller portion of their portfolio to speculative trades to capitalize on market opportunities. This balanced approach can help manage risk while providing room for growth, making it a comprehensive strategy for both conservative and aggressive investors.

Algorithmic Trading

Algorithmic trading is a game-changer in the stock market, offering a sharp departure from traditional trading methods. Instead of the old-school ways of buying and selling stocks or using futures and options, algorithmic trading uses complex algorithms and fast computers to place orders with incredible speed and accuracy.

This approach, also known as algo-trading, uses math-based models to make trading decisions at speeds no human can match, taking advantage of market opportunities that last only a split second. It's quite different from more traditional methods like investing in specific sectors or trading derivatives, which require more hands-on work and can be influenced by the traders' emotions and biases.

Growth of Algorithmic Trading in Indian Markets

Algorithmic trading has rapidly gained ground in the Indian stock market, propelled by technological advancements and increasing access to sophisticated trading tools. This trading method uses computer algorithms to make high-speed trading decisions based on market data analysis, enabling traders to execute orders at optimal prices and times.

The adoption of algorithmic trading in India has seen significant growth over the last decade. Initially, this growth was driven by institutional investors such as mutual funds, hedge funds, and proprietary trading firms. However, with advancements in technology and the democratization of trading tools, retail investors are increasingly turning to algorithmic trading to enhance their trading strategies.

One of the key factors contributing to the rise of algorithmic trading in India is the integration of artificial intelligence (AI) and machine learning (ML) with trading systems. These technologies enable algorithms to learn from market patterns and improve their predictions and decision-making processes over time, thereby increasing the efficiency and profitability of trades.

SEBI Regulations Governing Algorithmic Trading

As algorithmic trading gains traction in the Indian stock market, the Securities and Exchange Board of India (SEBI) plays a crucial role in shaping the landscape with a robust regulatory framework. SEBI's regulations ensure that all participants engaging in algorithmic trading adhere to stringent guidelines to maintain market integrity and fairness.

All brokers and firms must register their trading algorithms with the exchanges to verify compliance with trading norms and risk management requirements. This process includes detailed documentation of the algorithm's strategy and operational controls, which are subject to regular audits.

Before deployment, algorithms must undergo rigorous testing in simulated environments to ensure they do not destabilize the market. This includes checks for potential manipulative practices and the system's ability to handle sudden market movements. SEBI mandates that algorithms incorporate risk control measures like order limits and price collars to mitigate risks of market abuse.

Real-time monitoring systems are in place to oversee algorithmic trades, allowing regulators and exchanges to intervene promptly if irregular patterns emerge. Exchanges are equipped with 'kill switches' to halt trading activities that pose risks to market order.

SEBI emphasizes ethical trading practices, ensuring algorithms do not engage in manipulative strategies such as quote stuffing or spoofing. By maintaining these standards, SEBI not only protects the market but also boosts its efficiency and transparency, fostering confidence among all market participants.

This regulatory oversight by SEBI ensures that the Indian markets remain a level playing field for investors and that technological advancements in trading are harnessed responsibly and ethically.

As the Indian market continues to evolve, driven by technological advancements and regulatory enhancements, these investment strategies will not only grow in sophistication but also in accessibility. For retail investors and financial professionals alike, understanding and adapting to these methods will be crucial in achieving sustained financial success.

The evolution of trading practices, from manual to algorithmic, mirrors the broader transformation of global financial markets. By embracing these advancements, investors can look forward to harnessing the full potential of the Indian stock market, securing not just returns but a deeper understanding of the intricate dance of supply and demand that defines modern economics.

In this ever-changing financial landscape, the key to mastering the stock market lies in continuous learning and adaptability, ensuring that each investor can find the right balance between risk and reward according to their individual goals and market conditions.

Chapter 9

Overcoming Financial Setbacks

There was a time in my life when financial turmoil felt like a dark cloud that wouldn't lift, casting a long shadow over everything I did. It was during this challenging period that I stumbled upon a phrase by TD Jakes that struck a chord deep within me: "Every setback is a setup for a comeback." These words, simple yet profound, sparked a glimmer of hope in my weary heart.

Suddenly, the overwhelming burden of my financial struggles began to feel less like a permanent weight and more like a temporary obstacle. It dawned on me that overcoming these setbacks wasn't just a possibility—it was entirely within reach. All I needed was a blend of patience, diligence, and, most importantly, a robust strategy.

This realization was liberating. It wasn't about brushing off the setbacks or denying their impact. Instead, it was about acknowledging the struggle and understanding that with the right approach, I could navigate through it. This chapter is dedicated to everyone who has ever found themselves pinned under the heavy weight of financial distress. Together, we'll explore practical, actionable strategies to manage and overcome debt, learn from financial mistakes, and turn those setbacks into meaningful comebacks.

Whether you're dealing with the aftermath of a bad investment, the stress of accumulating debts, or the frustration of financial missteps, remember: you're not just fighting to get back to where you were. You're setting the stage for where you're going to be.

Strategies for Overcoming Debt and Financial Mistakes

Let's delve into one of the most practical aspects of regaining control over your finances: overcoming debt. As someone who has navigated through the murky waters of financial mishaps, I can vouch for the effectiveness of a structured approach to debt management. By breaking down the process into clear, actionable steps, I've found a way not just to manage debt, but to master it. Here's how you can do the same.

Step 1: List All Your Debts

Starting on the road to financial clarity means taking a simple but crucial first step: understanding your debt. It's more than just jotting down figures; it's about laying the groundwork for a detailed plan to take back control of your finances. Here's a guide to help you clearly and efficiently organize your debts:

Gather Documentation: Start by collecting every piece of documentation related to your debts. This includes your latest credit card statements, loan documents, and any other financial obligations that require regular payments. This paperwork is the raw data from which you will draw a complete picture of your financial obligations.

Create a Debt List: With all your documents at hand, create a centralized list of all your debts. You can use a simple spreadsheet or a specialized financial app to keep things organized. For each entry, make sure to note down the creditor's name, the total amount owed, the minimum monthly payment required, the interest rate, and the due date. This detailed list serves as the backbone of your debt repayment plan.

Verify Debets: The final step in this initial phase is to verify the accuracy of all the information. Cross-reference each debt entry with your credit reports to ensure there are no discrepancies or errors. Mistakes on your credit report can be common, and identifying them early can save you from potential setbacks on your journey to debt repayment.

When you take the time to list and check all your debts, what you're really doing is turning a messy heap of bills and statements into a neat and clear picture of your finances. Getting this clarity is super important—it gives you the power to make smart choices about how to tackle your debt and lays down a strong base for your next moves and strategies.

Step 2: Understand Interest Rates

Moving forward in our journey to regain financial control, the next pivotal step is to demystify the interest rates attached to your debts. Understanding this is not just about crunching numbers; it's about gaining insights that can profoundly influence your repayment strategy.

Types of Interest Rates: First, it's crucial to know the type of interest rate each of your debts carries. Are they fixed, meaning the rate doesn't change throughout the loan period? Or are they variable, fluctuating based on market conditions? This knowledge dictates how predictable your payments will be over time. Fixed rates offer stability, allowing you to plan with certainty, while variable rates introduce an element of unpredictability, which might affect your budgeting.

Calculate Total Interest: Here's where you need to roll up your sleeves a bit. Utilize online calculators to determine the total interest you'll pay over the life of each debt. This exercise isn't just about seeing numbers; it's about prioritizing which debts you should tackle first based on how much they're truly costing you. The higher the interest, the more urgent the need for repayment becomes to avoid costly long-term effects.

Impact of Compounding: Particularly critical with credit cards, the compounding of interest can turn what seems like manageable debt into a growing challenge. Compounding means that interest is calculated not only on your initial principal but also on the accumulated interest from previous periods. This can cause your debt to grow faster than you might expect, emphasizing the need for a strategic approach to payment that targets these high-compounding debts early in your repayment plan.

Step 3: Prioritize Repayments

Now that we have a clear understanding of your debts and the impact of those interest rates, let's focus on strategically tackling your repayments. This step is about optimizing how and when you pay to clear your debt efficiently and effectively.

Evaluate Payment Impact: Before diving into any specific strategy, assess how much of your payment is going towards the principal versus interest. This helps you understand which debts are merely keeping you in place versus which are bringing you closer to being debt-free. Focus on those debts where your payments effectively decrease the principal, which will reduce the total interest paid over time.

Boost Payment Frequency: Consider increasing the frequency of your payments. If your cash flow allows, switching from monthly to bi-weekly payments can have a significant impact. This approach reduces your interest over the lifespan of the debt and can also speed up the debt repayment process significantly.

Consider Debt Consolidation: If managing multiple high-interest debts becomes overwhelming, think about consolidating them into one loan with a lower interest rate. This can simplify your payment process and potentially reduce the amount you pay in interest, making your financial management more manageable.

Negotiate with Creditors: It's often possible to negotiate better terms with your creditors. Whether it's reducing the interest rate or adjusting repayment terms, creditors might be flexible if they believe it will increase their chances of getting repaid. Engaging in these negotiations can significantly alter your repayment strategy for the better.

Each payment is a step towards regaining financial freedom, crafted to ensure you're using your resources in the most effective way possible.

Step 4: Create a Budget and Payment Plan

The next step of our financial recovery revolves around something seemingly mundane yet incredibly powerful: crafting a precise budget and payment plan. This involves regaining control and steering your ship out of troubled waters with confidence.

Assess Your Income and Expenses: Start by laying out a clear map of your financial landscape. List every source of income and every expense. This isn't merely about seeing numbers; it's about understanding your financial flow. Identify areas where you might be overspending or where you can reasonably cut back. The goal here is to free up as much money as possible for debt repayment without compromising your basic needs. Think of this as fine-tuning your financial engine so it runs more efficiently.

Allocate Funds for Debt Repayment: With your streamlined budget, designate specific amounts towards your debts. Prioritize these payments, ensuring you cover at least the minimum required to avoid penalties. However, if your budget allows, aim to pay more than the minimum. This will reduce your principal faster and decrease the amount of interest you'll pay in the long run. Consider this allocation as an investment in your financial future—the more you can invest now, the quicker you'll be free from debt.

Set Up Reminders: In the digital age, we have tools at our fingertips that can keep us on track. Utilize calendar apps or set up automated reminders for each payment's due date. This simple step can help you avoid late fees and the stress that comes from missed payments. Think of these reminders as your personal financial assistants, nudging you at just the right moment to ensure every dollar goes exactly where it should.

Each step you take on this plan is a step away from debt and a step closer to reclaiming your financial independence.

Step 5: Monitor Progress and Adjust as Needed

As we move into the final stretch of regaining control over our financial lives, it's crucial to stay vigilant and adaptive. This isn't just a concluding phase—it's an ongoing process that ensures your financial strategy remains dynamic and responsive to your life's ever-changing circumstances.

Track Your Debt Reduction: Make it a regular habit to update and review your debt list. This isn't just about ticking boxes; it's about visualizing your journey towards financial freedom. Seeing the numbers decrease provides a concrete measure of your progress and keeps your motivation aflame. It's like watching the distance to a destination decrease on a road trip; each checkmark is a milestone in your journey towards a debt-free life.

Adjust Budget: Life is unpredictable, and financial situations can improve just as often as they can take a downturn. If you find yourself with increased income or unexpected financial gains, revisit your budget. See this as an opportunity to accelerate your debt repayment. Allocating extra funds towards your debts can significantly shorten your journey to becoming debt-free. Conversely, if your finances tighten, adjust your budget to maintain sustainability without derailing your debt repayment plan.

Celebrate Milestones: Every debt milestone you reach deserves recognition. Whether it's paying off a credit card, or reducing your total debt by a significant percentage, take a moment to celebrate these victories. These aren't just financial achievements; they're personal triumphs over your past constraints, reinforcing your capabilities and resilience. Celebrating these successes fuels your drive to continue, reminding you that every effort you make has real, tangible results.

This structured approach helped me tackle my debts and empowered me to seize control of my financial destiny. By embracing these steps, daunting financial challenges transform into manageable tasks, setting the path toward financial freedom. The journey to overcoming debt transcends mere repayment—it's an education, a growth process, and a journey towards becoming financially savvy.

Breaking the Chains of Debt- Methods for Effective Repayment

Now, let's zoom in on specific strategies for tackling debt. We'll start with a method that many find incredibly approachable and rewarding: the Snowball Method. This approach has not only helped countless individuals gain traction in their debt repayment journeys but has also transformed the overwhelming task of debt management into a series of manageable, motivating victories.

Snowball Method

The Snowball Method simplifies the debt repayment process by focusing on paying off your smallest debts first, then working your way up to the largest. You start with the most manageable piece, gaining momentum as each balance is wiped clean.

The true power of the Snowball Method lies in its psychological impact. Each debt cleared marks a win on your financial scoreboard, boosting your confidence and commitment. This method turns the daunting mountain of debt into a series of achievable hills, each one increasing your financial fitness and readiness to tackle the next.

One of the strongest advantages of the Snowball Method is how it enhances your motivation. Clearing smaller debts quickly provides tangible proof of progress. For many, this creates a psychological uplift that drives them to keep pushing forward, maintaining focus and adherence to their repayment plan.

The downside? It might cost you more in the long run. Since the focus is on the balance amount rather than the interest rate, higher interest debts sit longer, possibly accumulating additional interest.

Consider a compelling study from the Kellogg School of Management, which analyzed the debt repayment strategies of 6,000 consumers. The findings revealed that those employing the Snowball Method were more likely to clear their entire debt balance compared to others using different strategies. This underscores the method's psychological advantage, suggesting that the motivation gained from quick wins can be crucial in driving the completion of debt repayment.

Avalanche Method

Let's shift our focus to another effective strategy known as the Avalanche Method. This approach offers a more financially strategic route compared to the Snowball Method, focusing on minimizing the overall interest costs, which can lead to substantial savings over time.

The Avalanche Method tackles debt by prioritizing payments toward debts with the highest interest rates first, regardless of the balance size. This strategy is aimed at reducing the amount paid in interest, making it a cost-effective option for long-term financial health.

The challenge with the Avalanche Method lies in its psychological demands. Since it often targets larger or high-interest debts first, it can take a considerable amount of time before you see any debts fully paid off. This delay in visible progress can test your resolve and make it harder to stick to the plan, especially if you thrive on quick wins for motivation.

The most significant advantage of the Avalanche Method is the potential for substantial interest savings. By attacking the highest interest rates first, you minimize the cumulative interest, reducing overall costs. However, this method demands high discipline and patience. Without the frequent morale boosts of paying off smaller debts, maintaining momentum can be challenging.

Consider a real-life example highlighted by CNBC, where an individual with multiple debts—including a high-interest credit card debt at 22.24% APR—used the Avalanche Method. By focusing on this high-interest debt first, they significantly reduced the amount of interest accrued, resulting in considerable long-term savings compared to strategies like the Snowball Method.

Comparative Analysis

Interest Savings

The Avalanche Method often leads to lower total interest payments due to its focus on high-interest rates first. In contrast, while the Snowball Method may offer quicker psychological wins by clearing smaller balances, it typically results in higher total interest costs.

Motivational Factors

The Snowball Method's structure—clearing smaller debts first—provides immediate successes, which can be incredibly motivating and encourage adherence to the repayment plan. On the other hand, the Avalanche Method, focusing on interest rates, might discourage those who need frequent signs of progress to stay motivated.

Adherence and Success Rates

Research and practical experience suggest that the Snowball Method might enjoy higher success rates among users because its quick wins provide continuous motivation. However, from a mathematical standpoint, the Avalanche Method is superior in minimizing costs. The choice between these methods often depends on an individual's need for immediate results versus overall savings.

Deciding between the Snowball and Avalanche methods depends largely on personal preference, financial goals, and psychological makeup. If you're someone who gains momentum from seeing debts disappear quickly, the Snowball Method might suit you best. Conversely, if your focus is on reducing costs over time and you're comfortable with a slow but economically efficient process, the Avalanche Method could be the way to go. Both strategies have proven effective under different circumstances, and the best choice varies based on your unique financial situation and psychological needs.

Turning Financial Failures into Learning Opportunities

In the face of financial setbacks, I often remind myself of a powerful quote by Nelson Mandela: "I never lose. I either win or learn." This perspective has been a beacon during turbulent financial times, underscoring the importance of transforming every setback into a stepping stone. Let's explore how we can turn financial failures into invaluable learning opportunities, ensuring we emerge stronger and more financially astute.

Acknowledge and Analyze the Failure

Acceptance: The first step in overcoming a financial failure is acceptance. It's natural to feel disappointment or denial, but acknowledging the setback is crucial. This acceptance does not mean resignation; it means preparing to tackle the issue head-on. It's about shifting from a mindset of defeat to one of determination and growth.

Detailed Analysis: Once you've acknowledged the setback, it's time to dive deep and understand what went wrong. This involves a couple of critical steps:

Identifying the Trigger: What kicked off this financial setback? Was it a drop in the market, a risky investment that didn't pan out, or perhaps an unexpected financial emergency? Pinpointing the trigger is the first step in understanding the failure.

Understanding the Impact: Next, assess how this setback has affected your financial health. Look at the immediate effects, such as cash flow interruptions or increased debt levels, and consider the long-term impacts, like potential hits to your credit score or savings goals. Understanding the scope of the impact helps in planning an effective recovery strategy.

Gather Data and Insights

Financial Review: Go through your financial statements, investment reports, and budget records meticulously. Analyze the decisions that led up to the failure. This is not about assigning blame, but about gaining a clear and unbiased understanding of your financial habits and decisions.

Market and Environmental Factors: Consider external factors that might have influenced your financial situation. Economic downturns, sudden market changes, and new regulations can all play significant roles in financial setbacks. Recognizing these factors can help in recalibrating your expectations and strategies moving forward.

Feedback and Advice: This is a good time to consult with financial advisors or mentors. Their professional insights can shed light on aspects of the situation you might have missed and can guide you in adjusting your financial strategies effectively.

Learning from the Setback

Every financial setback holds key lessons that can forge stronger future strategies. For instance, if a sudden market downturn impacted your investments, the key takeaway might be the critical importance of diversification. Perhaps your portfolio was too heavily weighted in a volatile sector, suggesting a need to spread out risk more broadly across different asset types.

It's essential to keep a written record of what you've learned. Writing down these insights helps cement the lessons and creates a valuable reference for future decision-making. This documentation acts as a guidebook for navigating similar challenges ahead, ensuring you remember and apply what you've learned when it matters most.

Strategic Adjustment

With these lessons in hand, take a moment to reassess and adjust your financial goals. Maybe you've realized the need for a more substantial emergency fund or the importance of reducing your debt load to increase financial stability. Adjust your goals to better prepare you for future fluctuations, making your financial foundation more robust.

Now, realign your financial plans to fit these updated goals. This could mean shifting your investment strategies to include more conservative or diverse options, revising your budget to allocate more towards savings, or setting stricter criteria for future expenditures. Each adjustment is a step towards making your financial landscape more resilient.

Finally, bolster your risk management strategies. Depending on the nature of your previous setback, this might involve purchasing additional insurance, such as income protection or critical illness cover, or perhaps adjusting your investment portfolio to include assets that perform well in different market conditions. This proactive approach not only safeguards your assets but also gives you peace of mind.

Implementation and Monitoring

Action Plan: Now that we've reshaped our financial goals and adjusted our strategies, it's time to create a detailed action plan. This should outline specific steps you need to take, assign responsibilities—whether to yourself or to a financial advisor—and set realistic timelines for each task. Having a clear, actionable plan helps translate your strategic adjustments into daily practices and decisions.

Regular Reviews: Financial landscapes are dynamic, influenced by personal life changes, economic shifts, and global events. To ensure your financial plan remains effective and aligned with your goals, establish a routine for regularly reviewing it. This might be quarterly, semi-annually, or annually, depending on your situation. These reviews are pivotal in assessing the plan's effectiveness and making necessary adjustments to stay on course.

Adaptability: If there's one certainty in finance, it's uncertainty. Maintaining flexibility within your financial planning is essential. This flexibility allows you to adapt swiftly to unexpected circumstances—be it a sudden financial opportunity or an unforeseen expense—without significantly derailing your overall strategy.

Building Resilience

Continuous Learning: The world of finance is ever-evolving, and staying informed is key to maintaining a robust financial strategy. Engage in ongoing education, whether through formal courses, reading up on the latest financial insights, or participating in workshops. This continuous learning not only enhances your financial literacy but also empowers you to make informed decisions.

Stress Testing: To truly test the resilience of your financial strategies, periodically simulate potential adverse scenarios. How would your finances hold up in a market downturn? What if there was a sudden major expense? These stress tests can help you evaluate the robustness of your plan and pinpoint areas that need strengthening.

Community and Support Networks: No one should navigate their financial journey alone. Building a network of knowledgeable and trustworthy individuals—professionals, peers, mentors—can provide substantial support. This community can offer guidance, share insights, and provide encouragement through financial ups and downs. Their collective wisdom is an invaluable asset that can help you steer through challenges more effectively.

By taking these steps, you're fixing past financial hiccups and you're also setting the stage for future triumphs. Every move you make is a stride towards stability, insight, and unshakeable resilience.

How Can You Bulletproof Your Finances Against Future Setbacks?

After patching up those past money mishaps, the big question that hits you next is, "How do we make sure this mess doesn't happen again? How can we armor our finances against future bumps?" Well, here are some smart moves to include safety nets and flexibility into your financial game plan, helping you stand strong against whatever comes next.

Strategic Use of Financial Instruments for Flexibility

Liquidity Management: It's wise to keep a portion of your investments in liquid assets. This ensures you have quick access to funds in emergencies without substantial losses. Liquid assets can act as a financial lifeline when unexpected expenses arise.

Flexible Investment Vehicles: Utilize versatile investment tools such as exchange-traded funds (ETFs) and mutual funds. These can be easily adjusted or liquidated without heavy penalties, providing an essential buffer that allows you to respond swiftly to market changes or personal financial shifts.

Dynamic Risk Management Strategies

Regular Risk Assessments: Continually assess your risk exposure and adjust your strategies to align with current financial conditions. This includes revisiting insurance coverage levels and the risk profile of your investments to ensure they match your evolving financial situation.

Diversification Across Asset Classes: Spreading your investments across various asset classes (stocks, bonds, real estate, etc.) helps mitigate risks associated with market volatility. Diversification acts as a risk buffer, smoothing out the peaks and troughs of investment performance.

Use of Derivatives for Hedging: For those with more complex financial portfolios, consider financial derivatives like options and futures to hedge against market downturns. These instruments can provide peace of mind by protecting against significant market corrections.

Building an Emergency Fund

Sizing Your Emergency Fund: Aim to maintain an emergency fund that covers 3-6 months of living expenses. This fund should be readily accessible, possibly in a high-yield savings account, ensuring that you can meet unexpected financial demands without disrupting your long-term investment strategy.

Incremental Savings Strategy: Establish automatic monthly transfers to your emergency fund from your primary account. This systematic approach ensures your emergency fund grows steadily without needing constant attention.

Incorporating Insurance in Financial Planning

Comprehensive Coverage: Comprehensive insurance coverage—including health, life, disability, and property—is essential. These policies protect you from potentially devastating financial impacts of unexpected events.

Review and Adjust Coverage: Regularly review your insurance policies to ensure they remain aligned with your current financial circumstances and provide adequate coverage.

Flexible Financial Goals and Retirement Planning

Adjustable Financial Goals: Set flexible financial goals that can adapt to changes in your financial landscape. For instance, if market conditions dampen investment returns, be prepared to adjust your savings goals or retirement planning timeline accordingly.

Retirement Contributions Flexibility: Opt for retirement accounts that offer flexible contribution options. This flexibility can be crucial during times when financial circumstances change, allowing you to adjust contributions without penalties.

Use of Technology and Financial Tools

Financial Planning Software: Leverage advanced financial planning software to monitor investments, track expenses, and project financial goals. Many of these tools include scenario planning features that help you prepare for different financial outcomes.

Mobile Budgeting Apps: Utilize mobile budgeting apps that integrate with your financial accounts. These apps provide real-time insights into your spending and saving patterns, allowing for immediate adjustments.

Continuous Education and Professional Advice

Stay Informed: Regularly update your financial knowledge by following current market trends and financial advice. This ongoing education helps you stay prepared for both opportunities and potential threats.

Consult with Financial Advisors: An experienced financial advisor can offer personalized insights and adjustments to your financial strategy, tailored to your specific circumstances and goals.

When you integrate these all-encompassing strategies into your financial plan, you're building a strong safety net that protects you from life's curveballs while keeping you nimble enough to adapt with change. It's like giving your finances a present and future-proof armor.

Comeback Stories in Finance

As we delve into the transformative power of overcoming financial distress, I'm continually inspired by the real-life stories of individuals who have risen from challenging circumstances. One such story that has profoundly impacted me is that of Sharita M. Humphrey, a finance expert and money mentor whose journey from hardship to financial independence embodies the essence of determination and strategic financial planning.

Several years ago, Sharita found herself in a dire situation: she was a homeless single mom with two small children, forced to live in a motel after being evicted. With no savings and a plummeting credit score due to eviction and outstanding debts, including credit and medical bills, her prospects seemed bleak. But Sharita knew surrender was not an option—not with two young children depending on her.

Determined to change her circumstances, Sharita embarked on a journey to enhance her financial literacy. She and her children became regular visitors at their local public library, where she immersed herself in personal development and finance books. Sharita's commitment to learning laid the foundation for her financial turnaround.

She carefully began to map out her goals, establishing a straightforward budget and dedicating a portion of her paycheck to savings each month. Step by step, she worked on rebuilding her credit and eliminating her debts. This journey was far from easy; it demanded persistence and a steadfast belief in her ability to secure a better future for her family.

Her efforts bore fruit as she gradually regained financial stability and confidence. Eventually, Sharita and her children moved into their new home, and she secured a government job, which she later left to launch her own company. Through her experience, Sharita became a ray of hope and guidance for others in similar situations, advocating for the importance of never losing hope and the power of a shifted mindset.

Sharita's journey shines a bright light on the transformative power of financial smarts. Armed with budgeting discipline and an unwavering positive attitude, she turned her life around.

Her journey reminds us all that change is possible when you commit to understanding your finances, setting clear goals, and persistently working towards them, regardless of the obstacles.

Another compelling story of resilience and financial recovery is that Dhirubhai Ambani. His journey from a modest village in Gujarat to founding Reliance Industries is more than a success story—it's a testament to the transformative power of vision and tenacity. His life offers profound insights into building an empire against the odds and reshaping an economy.

Born into a family where making ends meet was a daily challenge, Ambani's early life was marked by simplicity and scarcity. But even in his youth, his ambitions were anything but simple. At 16, he took a bold step by moving to Yemen, where he worked at a gas station. This job, seemingly mundane, was his first classroom in the world of business, teaching him invaluable lessons about commerce and customer service.

Returning to India with dreams bigger than his pockets could initially fund, Ambani didn't dive straight into wealth. He started small—a trading business that slowly but steadily grew. He lived by a principle that later defined his empire: "Pursue your goals even in the face of difficulties, and convert adversities into opportunities."

Strategic Insights from Ambani's Rise

Innovative Thinking: Ambani was quick to recognize the potential of the burgeoning textile industry. He ventured into manufacturing polyester fibers, which at the time was a bold and innovative move. His willingness to embrace new ideas and technologies gave him an edge in a competitive market.

Resource Leveraging: His journey wasn't a solo venture. His family provided crucial support, both emotionally and financially, which helped him navigate the early and turbulent waters of business setup. He also wasn't shy about using loans strategically to scale his operations—understanding that timely investment could lead to exponential growth.

Building Resilience: Ambani's path wasn't without its hurdles. He faced intense competition, market volatility, and even natural disasters that threatened his factories. Each time, his response wasn't just to endure but to emerge stronger, turning each crisis into a stepping stone for further growth.

Cultivating Skills and Team Building: Knowing that a visionary leader needs a capable team, Ambani focused on attracting and nurturing talent. He invested in training programs, fostering a culture of innovation and dedication that would drive his company forward.

Ambani's life teaches us that substantial financial success is accessible with the right mix of perseverance, strategic planning, and an adaptive mindset. He demonstrated that:

- Learning from every opportunity can provide the foundation for massive future success.
- Strategic investment and resource management are pillars of building and sustaining a business.

- Facing challenges with resilience can transform potential setbacks into opportunities for growth.

Dhirubhai Ambani inspired a nation. His story is a powerful reminder that with belief in one's vision and the courage to pursue it relentlessly, transforming financial struggles into remarkable success is not merely possible—it's achievable.

As we explore the various facets of overcoming financial setbacks, it's important to recognize that each story of recovery and each piece of advice is more than just a roadmap to financial stability—it upholds human resilience and adaptability.

Financial setbacks, while daunting, are not the end of the story. They are, in fact, pivotal chapters that test our strategies, beliefs, and endurance. How we respond to these challenges can redefine our financial narratives, turning potential defeats into defining victories. The key lies in our willingness to learn, adapt, and persevere.

As you reflect on the strategies and stories shared, consider how you might apply these lessons to your own financial challenges. What aspects of your financial plan could benefit from a more resilient and flexible approach? How can you turn today's setbacks into tomorrow's comebacks? And most importantly, how can you transform your relationship with money in a way that not only secures your financial future but also aligns with your values and life goals?

Chapter 10

Retirement Readiness

Imagine this scene: a retired couple sipping their morning tea on a serene balcony in Pune, overlooking a lush garden. They chat about the day's plans with no rush to head out the door. This peace of mind comes from years of prudent planning and wise investments, particularly in government-backed retirement schemes.

Retirement readiness goes beyond simple financial planning; it involves comprehensive preparation for a stable and fulfilling post-retirement life. It means securing enough resources not just for survival, but for flourishing, allowing you to enjoy activities you may have delayed due to work and family obligations.

At its core, retirement readiness involves a deep understanding of what you'll need to live comfortably after you stop working. It includes planning for expenses like healthcare, which often increases with age, housing needs, daily living costs, and even leisure activities that make life enjoyable. This readiness isn't just about accumulating a large sum of money but about strategically planning how that money is saved, invested, and eventually spent.

A well-rounded retirement plan considers several factors:

- **Longevity:** With life expectancies rising, your retirement funds may need to last 20 to 30 years or more. Planning for a longer life means ensuring you won't outlive your savings.

- **Inflation:** The cost of living will rise over time. A loaf of bread costs more today than it did twenty years ago, and the same will hold true two decades from now. Effective retirement planning accounts for this gradual increase in prices, ensuring your purchasing power isn't eroded.

- **Healthcare Needs:** As we age, healthcare becomes a more significant expense. Planning for medical costs, including potential long-term care, is critical in retirement planning.

- **Lifestyle Goals:** Retirement is a time to pursue passions that work may have pushed to the sidelines. Whether it's travel, hobbies, or social activities, considering these in your retirement budget is essential for a fulfilling post-work life.

This chapter is dedicated to guiding you toward a similarly secure retirement. In India, where family ties are strong and traditions run deep, preparing for retirement is more than a personal journey—it's a way to ensure you continue to thrive without compromising on lifestyle or responsibilities.

Understanding the Basics

We'll start by examining three cornerstone retirement schemes: the Employees' Provident Fund (EPF), Public Provident Fund (PPF), and National Pension System (NPS). Each offers unique benefits and is tailored to different retirement needs and stages of your career.

Employees' Provident Fund (EPF)

The EPF is a retirement benefit scheme that's available to all salaried employees in India, and it's managed by the Employees' Provident Fund Organization (EPFO). Every company with more than 20 employees is required to register with the EPFO. Here's how it works: both the employee and employer contribute 12% of the employee's basic salary plus dearness allowance to the EPF account each month. Employees can contribute more if they choose, which is known as Voluntary Provident Fund contributions. The current interest rate for EPF accounts is 8.25% per annum, compounded monthly.

Let's consider Sunita, a software developer earning ₹30,000 monthly. Both she and her employer contribute ₹3,600 each month to her EPF account. The interest rate as of now is 8.25% per annum, compounded monthly, making it a robust savings mechanism for her retirement. The total accumulated amount in her EPF can significantly grow over the years, providing a substantial sum upon retirement.

Public Provident Fund (PPF)

The PPF is a popular long-term savings scheme open to all Indian citizens, not just salaried employees. It's particularly favored for its tax-saving potential, as contributions, interest earned, and withdrawals are all tax-exempt under Section 80C of the Income Tax Act. The PPF has a tenure of 15 years, which can be extended in blocks of five years. The interest rate is reviewed and announced by the government quarterly, and as of the latest update, it stands at about 7.1% per annum.

For example, Rohan, a freelance graphic designer, contributes ₹1,20,000 annually to his PPF. With an interest rate of approximately 7.1% per annum, compounded yearly, his investment not only grows but also offers tax benefits under Section 80C. After the mandatory lock-in period of 15 years, Rohan can either withdraw the full amount tax-free or extend it in blocks of five years.

National Pension System (NPS)

The NPS is a more recent addition, introduced to provide a sustainable solution to provide retirement income. It is available to all Indian citizens between the ages of 18 and 65. The NPS allows subscribers to contribute regularly in a pension account during their working life. On retirement, subscribers can withdraw a part of the corpus in a lump sum and use the remaining amount to buy an annuity to secure a regular income after retirement. The NPS is unique because it invests in a mix of securities such as government bonds, bills, corporate debentures, and shares depending on the subscriber's choice, which can potentially offer higher returns compared to EPF and PPF.

Anjali, a corporate executive, opts for a higher equity allocation in her early career to maximize growth. She contributes ₹10,000 monthly to her NPS account. By the time she retires, a portion of her corpus can be withdrawn as a lump sum, and the remainder is used to purchase an annuity, ensuring a regular pension income. NPS's flexible structure allows Anjali to adjust her investment choices based on her risk appetite and life stage.

Enrollment and Eligibility

- **EPF:** Mandatory for salaried employees in firms with over 20 workers, with an option for firms with fewer employees to join voluntarily. The mandatory salary ceiling for EPF contribution is ₹15,000 per month, but employees earning above this amount can also opt to contribute with the consent of their employer and approval from the Assistant PF Commissioner.
- **PPF:** Open to all Indian citizens. It can be opened at a nationalized bank or post office with a minimum yearly deposit of ₹500 and a maximum of ₹1,50,000.
- **NPS:** Open to all Indian citizens aged between 18 and 65. Subscribers can contribute to their NPS accounts through various modes and change the amount of contribution as per their financial capability.

These schemes form the backbone of retirement savings for millions of Indians, providing financial security through their structured approach to long-term savings and investment. Each has its own set of rules regarding eligibility, contributions, and benefits, tailored to meet the diverse needs of the Indian populace from various employment sectors.

Introduction to Creating a Diversified Retirement Portfolio

A well-rounded retirement portfolio is much like a balanced diet—each component plays a crucial role in maintaining overall health and achieving long-term goals. Just as you wouldn't rely solely on one type of food for nutrition, relying on a single investment type can leave your retirement savings vulnerable to market volatility. Diversifying across various asset classes such as equities, debt, gold, and real estate helps mitigate these risks and optimize returns, ensuring a more stable financial future.

Diversification is a fundamental investment strategy aimed at minimizing risk while maximizing potential returns by spreading investments across various asset classes. Each asset class—equity, debt, gold, and real estate—carries its own set of risks and rewards, and their performance can vary under different economic conditions. By diversifying your portfolio, you can protect it against significant fluctuations in any single asset class.

Equity

Equities or stocks represent ownership in a company and offer high return potential relative to other asset classes. However, they also come with higher volatility and risk, especially in the short term. Over the long term, equities have historically provided significant capital appreciation and dividends, which are particularly beneficial for building a retirement corpus.

Debt

Debt investments, such as bonds or fixed deposits, provide regular income through interest payments. They are generally considered safer than equities because they offer lower volatility and a fixed income stream, making them a crucial part of a retirement portfolio, especially for those nearing retirement who may not have the tolerance for high risk.

Gold

Gold is often considered a 'safe haven' during periods of economic uncertainty. It can act as a hedge against inflation and currency devaluation, thereby adding a layer of security to your retirement savings. While it does not offer dividends or interest, its price appreciation over time can contribute to portfolio growth.

Real Estate

Real estate investments can offer both capital appreciation and rental income, making them a valuable component of a diversified portfolio. They are generally less volatile than equities and can provide a hedge against inflation, as property values and rents tend to rise with inflation.

Example of Diversification in Practice

Consider the hypothetical example of Meena, who is planning for her retirement. By allocating her investments across these four asset classes, she can achieve a balanced portfolio:

- *60% in Equities:* Targeting growth through stocks and equity mutual funds.
- *20% in Debt:* Using government bonds and corporate debentures for stability and regular income.
- *10% in Gold:* Adding a commodity element to hedge against inflation and economic uncertainty.
- *10% in Real Estate:* Investing in property to benefit from rental income and long-term appreciation.

This diversified approach helps Meena manage risks across her portfolio. When the stock market is down, her debt investments and real estate can provide stability and continue generating income, and vice versa.

Selecting Mutual Funds and Annuities for Retirement Savings

When planning for retirement, choosing the right investment vehicles is crucial. Mutual funds and annuities can be excellent choices for generating and stabilizing income during retirement. Here's how to assess these options to ensure they align with your financial goals.

Selecting Mutual Funds

Mutual funds pool money from many investors to purchase a diversified portfolio of stocks, bonds, or other securities. Here's how to select the right mutual fund for retirement savings:

- **Assess Your Risk Tolerance:** Understanding your risk tolerance is crucial. If you're closer to retirement, you might prefer debt mutual funds for more stable returns. Younger investors might opt for equity funds for higher growth potential.
- **Look at Historical Performance:** While past performance is not an indicator of future results, it can provide insights into how the fund has managed volatility and delivered returns over different market cycles.
- **Check the Expense Ratio:** Funds with high expense ratios can eat into your returns. Choosing funds with

lower costs can significantly impact your savings over time.

- **Fund Manager's Track Record:** Evaluate the experience and track record of the fund manager in managing the fund, especially during downturns.
- **Investment Strategy:** Ensure the fund's investment strategy aligns with your retirement goals. Some funds might focus on capital preservation while others on capital appreciation.

Suppose Neeta is 50 and wants a mix of stability and growth. She might allocate 70% of her retirement savings to a conservative hybrid mutual fund that invests in both stocks and bonds, and 30% to a high-quality short-duration debt fund, ensuring she has a balance of safety and modest growth.

Selecting Annuities

Annuities are insurance products that can provide a steady income stream during retirement. Here's how to evaluate them:

- **Type of Annuity:** Decide whether a fixed, variable, or indexed annuity suits your needs. Fixed annuities provide regular payments, while variable and indexed annuities offer payments tied to the performance of investments or indexes.
- **Payout Options:** Determine if you need immediate payouts or if you can wait (deferred annuities). Immediate annuities are suitable for those nearing or at retirement age.

- **Fees and Charges:** Understand all associated costs, which can vary widely among annuity providers. High fees can undermine the benefits of an annuity.
- **Financial Strength of the Insurer:** The insurer's financial strength is crucial as it impacts their ability to make payments. Check ratings from agencies like AM Best or Standard & Poor's.

Raj is looking to retire in five years and wants a guaranteed income post-retirement. He opts for an immediate fixed annuity with a reputable insurer that offers a competitive rate, ensuring a steady and predictable income stream to cover his basic expenses.

By carefully evaluating mutual funds and annuities, you can create a retirement portfolio that not only grows over time but also provides the financial security needed in your retirement years. This balanced approach allows you to enjoy your retirement comfortably, with peace of mind regarding your financial stability.

Real Estate as Retirement Investment

Investing in real estate is a popular strategy for retirement planning, offering potential for both income through rental yields and capital appreciation. However, like any investment, it comes with its set of advantages and challenges.

Pros of Investing in Real Estate for Retirement

- **Steady Income Stream:** Real estate can provide a regular rental income, which can be particularly appealing for retirees seeking a steady cash flow. This income can help cover living expenses and reduce the dependency on withdrawals from other retirement accounts.

- **Capital Appreciation:** Over time, real estate properties generally appreciate in value. This appreciation can significantly boost the total value of a retirement portfolio, offering a cushion against inflation and increasing the wealth that can be passed on to heirs.
- **Tax Advantages:** Real estate investors can benefit from various tax deductions related to property ownership, including mortgage interest, property taxes, and expenses from managing and maintaining the property.

Cons of Investing in Real Estate for Retirement

- **Liquidity Concerns:** Real estate is not as liquid as stocks or bonds. Selling a property can take considerable time, and the market conditions at the time of sale significantly affect the realizable value. This makes it less ideal for those who may need quick access to funds.
- **Maintenance and Management:** Owning property requires ongoing maintenance and management, which can be burdensome for retirees. The costs associated with repairs, upgrades, and property management services can erode potential returns.
- **Market Risk:** While real estate generally appreciates over time, market fluctuations can lead to periods of stagnation or even depreciation. Local market conditions heavily influence real estate values, making thorough research and strategic buying essential.

Rental Yield vs. Appreciation

When considering real estate as a retirement investment, it's crucial to balance the potential for rental yields against the prospects for appreciation:

- **Rental Yield:** This is the annual rental income from the property divided by the property's value, expressed as a percentage. A high rental yield can provide a good income stream, but high-yielding properties might not appreciate as quickly as those in more desirable locations.

- **Appreciation:** Appreciation refers to an increase in the property's value over time. While this can result in significant gains when the property is sold, betting solely on appreciation is riskier, especially if the property's location falls out of favor or the local real estate market declines.

Consider a retiree, Arjun, who buys a duplex in a growing suburb. The rental income covers his monthly mortgage payments and contributes a bit extra towards his living expenses. Over 20 years, the suburb develops significantly, increasing the property's value. Arjun's investment provides both a stable income during his retirement and a valuable asset for his estate.

Real estate can be a worthwhile addition to a retirement portfolio if managed wisely. It requires balancing the immediate benefits of rental income with the long-term potential for appreciation, all while considering the implications of liquidity and market risk. Careful selection and management of property can help retirees achieve a balanced and financially secure retirement.

Use Online Retirement Calculators Effectively

Online retirement calculators are invaluable tools that can help you plan for a financially secure retirement by providing insights into how much you need to save and how long your savings might last. Here's how to use these calculators effectively, including examples of popular calculators and tools.

How to Use Online Retirement Calculators Effectively

Retirement calculators come in different types, each designed to suit specific planning needs:

- **Basic Retirement Savings Calculators:** These calculators are straightforward and ideal for getting a quick snapshot of how much you need to save based on your age, desired retirement age, current savings, and expected annual return.
- **Comprehensive Retirement Planners:** These tools are more detailed and consider additional factors like expected Social Security benefits (or equivalent), other income sources, and varying expenses across different retirement phases.
- **Monte Carlo Simulation Tools:** These calculators use advanced statistical techniques to simulate a wide range of economic outcomes, helping you understand the probability of achieving your retirement goals under varying market conditions.

For example, calculators like the one from HDFC Life and INDMoney offer step-by-step guidance where you input your age, income details, and desired retirement age, among other financial details, to get a comprehensive view of your retirement planning needs.

Features of Effective Retirement Planning Tools

Effective retirement planning tools offer features that allow you to:

- Customize inputs to reflect your personal financial situation, such as monthly expenses, income growth rate, current investments, and retirement age.
- Perform scenario analysis to see how changes in investment returns, inflation rates, and savings contributions could affect your retirement plan.
- Receive suggestions on how much to save monthly and the best investment strategies to meet your retirement goals.
- Popular tools like those provided by Groww and Scripbox not only help calculate the required retirement corpus but also guide investment decisions by recommending appropriate mutual funds or other investment options suited for long-term growth and retirement planning.

Practical Usage Example

Suppose Anita, a 40-year-old with an annual income of ₹1,200,000, wants to retire at 65. She currently has ₹5,000,000 saved and contributes ₹100,000 annually to her retirement savings. Using a retirement calculator, she inputs these details along with expected annual raises of 2%, an inflation rate of 3%, and an investment return rate of 6%.

The calculator might project that Anita will accumulate approximately ₹40,000,000 by her retirement age, suggesting whether this will be sufficient based on her expected lifestyle and expenses in retirement. If the projection falls short of her needs, she could explore scenarios like increasing her annual savings or delaying her retirement age to improve her financial outlook.

Using Calculators for Scenario Analysis

- **Change Variables:** Experiment with different variables, such as higher or lower return rates, different retirement ages, and varying savings rates, to see how these changes affect your retirement planning.

- **Consider Life Changes:** Retirement calculators can also simulate major life changes like buying a home or receiving inheritance money, helping you understand their potential impacts on your retirement plans.

Examples of Effective Retirement Planning Software

- **Personal Capital:** This app provides a comprehensive financial management platform, combining investment tracking with advanced retirement planning features. It uses real-world data to project future balances and offers insights into how adjustments in savings or expenses might impact retirement goals.

- **Fidelity's myPlan Snapshot:** A straightforward tool that allows users to enter basic financial data—age, income, savings, and investment values—to get a quick overview of their retirement readiness. It provides visual representations of projected asset growth and potential income in retirement (MoneyWise).

- **New Retirement:** Known for its detailed approach, this platform allows users to create a highly customized retirement plan. It considers various income sources, housing equity, and different expense types, providing a comprehensive view of retirement planning (MoneyWise).

Chapter 11

Legacy and Generational Wealth

Generational wealth isn't just about assets, but also the values and wisdom passed down through generations. In India, where family and tradition are highly valued, managing wealth across generations is both a privilege and a serious duty. Stories of family businesses lasting centuries, lands nourishing families for generations, and evolving practices paint a vivid picture of the challenges and rewards of maintaining generational wealth.

The key to keeping generational wealth is creating a clear family wealth vision that matches shared values and long-term goals. This vision helps guide financial decisions and legacy planning, making sure every family member is working towards the same goal.

Steps to Create a Unified Family Wealth Vision

- **Family Meetings:** Regular family meetings are essential. They provide a platform for discussing financial matters, individual aspirations, and collective goals. These meetings foster transparency and allow every family member to feel involved and responsible for the family's legacy.
- **Define Shared Values:** What values do you want your wealth to promote? Is it entrepreneurship, philanthropy, education, or sustainability? Defining these values can

help align your family's wealth management strategies with broader, more meaningful objectives.

- **Set Long-Term Goals:** Whether it's expanding the family business, ensuring quality education for all descendants, or contributing to community development, setting clear and achievable goals is crucial. These goals should reflect the family's values and vision, providing a clear path forward.
- **Educate and Involve the Next Generation:** Integrating younger family members into discussions about wealth management from an early age prepares them to handle responsibilities in the future. This includes education on financial literacy, investments, and the ethical considerations of wealth stewardship.

These foundational steps enable families to manage their wealth effectively, ensuring that it not only grows but also supports the family's collective vision and values.

The Role of Life Insurance in Wealth Preservation

Life insurance plays a pivotal role in comprehensive estate planning, serving not just as a tool for financial protection but also as a strategic asset in the management and transition of wealth to future generations. Different types of life insurance policies, each with unique features, can be effectively integrated into a broader wealth preservation strategy.

Life insurance provides several critical benefits that can be harnessed to safeguard and manage family wealth:

- **Liquidity to Pay Estate Taxes:** Upon the death of an estate holder, significant taxes can be levied on inherited assets. Life insurance provides the liquidity necessary to handle these taxes without the need to sell off valuable assets or dip into other savings. This can be especially crucial for preserving the integrity of a business or family property that has emotional or strategic value.

- **Equalizing Inheritances:** In families where assets like a business or real estate are to be passed to one child, life insurance can help provide equitable treatment to other children. This is done by using the death benefit from the policy to offer a comparable inheritance to other heirs, thus maintaining harmony and fairness within the family structure.

- **Funding Buy-Sell Agreements:** In the context of family businesses, life insurance is invaluable in funding buy-sell agreements. Upon the death of a business owner, life insurance proceeds can be used to purchase the deceased owner's interest. This arrangement ensures that the business remains in the family or with designated co-owners, while also providing the deceased's family with fair compensation.

Types of Life Insurance Policies Used in Estate Planning

- **Whole Life Insurance:** This type of insurance not only provides a death benefit but also includes an investment component known as the cash value, which grows tax-deferred over time. Whole life insurance is particularly appealing for estate planning because it offers guaranteed cash value growth and life-long coverage.

- **Universal Life Insurance:** Universal life offers more flexibility than whole life insurance. It allows policyholders to adjust their premiums and death benefits over time to match their changing financial circumstances. This adaptability makes it suitable for more complex estate planning needs where financial situations are expected to evolve.
- **Variable Universal Life Insurance:** Combining the features of universal life with the ability to invest the cash value in various accounts, variable universal life can provide higher potential returns but also comes with higher risk. This policy is suitable for those who are more investment-savvy and willing to take on market risks to increase their estate value.

Integrating Life Insurance into Estate Planning

For effective integration, it is crucial to work with estate planning professionals who can provide tailored advice based on the family's financial situation and goals. For instance, if a family owns a substantial estate with expected high estate taxes, a financial planner might recommend a whole life policy with a high death benefit to ensure sufficient liquidity for tax obligations.

The Importance of Financial Education for Children and Teens

Educating children and teens about finances is crucial for preparing them to make wise financial decisions in adulthood. Early financial education helps instill a sense of financial responsibility and understanding that can contribute significantly to long-term personal and generational wealth management.

The approach to financial education should vary depending on the age and developmental stage of the child or teen. This ensures that the information is both understandable and relevant, making the learning process more effective and engaging.

- **Young Children (Ages 5-8):** For young children, the focus should be on basic concepts such as saving, the value of money, and simple budgeting. Activities like saving in a piggy bank, setting small saving goals (e.g., saving to buy a toy), and using simple, fun games that incorporate money can be very effective.

- **Pre-Teens (Ages 9-12):** At this stage, children can handle slightly more complex concepts such as compound interest, basic investment principles, and the importance of financial planning. Introducing allowances and encouraging them to manage their own money can teach budgeting and saving. Tools like basic financial apps designed for children can be introduced to simulate savings and check spending habits.

- **Teenagers (Ages 13-18):** Teenagers are ready to understand and manage more complex financial tasks such as setting long-term saving goals, basics of investing in stocks or bonds, and even concepts like credit scores and taxes. Encouraging teens to manage a small stock portfolio, perhaps through a simulation or a controlled environment with real money, can provide practical experience. Teaching them to budget their income from part-time jobs and discussing college savings are also crucial at this stage.

Implementing effective financial education often involves a combination of home-based learning and formal educational programs. Schools can integrate financial literacy into the curriculum through dedicated classes or as part of math and economics courses. At home, parents can use real-life experiences such as family budgeting sessions, shopping trips, or financial planning for vacations to teach practical financial skills.

Several tools and resources can enhance financial education:

- **Educational Apps and Games:** Apps like 'Bankaroo' for young children or 'Renegade Buggies' designed by the National Center for Families Learning can make learning about savings and spending fun and practical.
- **Online Courses and Workshops:** Organizations like the National Endowment for Financial Education offer workshops and resources tailored to teenagers, covering topics from college planning to managing personal finances.
- **Books and Interactive Media:** Books such as "The Kids' Money Book" by Jamie Kyle McGillian provide a great way to discuss financial concepts. Interactive websites like Biz Kid$ help explain complex financial concepts in a teen-friendly manner.

Through strategic planning, as discussed in the sections on unified family wealth visions, estate planning, and life insurance, families can protect and perpetuate their legacies.

Each tool and strategy is not merely about securing assets but about laying a foundation that future generations can build upon. As we've seen, life insurance can bridge financial gaps and provide security, while robust estate planning ensures that assets are transferred smoothly and in alignment with the family's wishes.

Furthermore, the role of financial education cannot be overstated. By instilling a sense of financial literacy in children and teens, we prepare them not just to inherit wealth but to expand it responsibly.

Conclusion

As we reach the final pages of our journey to wealth maximization, it's time to reflect on the knowledge we've gained and the steps we've taken together. In the words of Ayn Rand, "Wealth is the product of a man's capacity to think." This journey has been about expanding our thinking, shifting our practices, and equipping ourselves with the tools to achieve financial success.

Let's revisit some of the core strategies and principles we've explored:

Understanding Assets and Liabilities: Recognizing what you own versus what you owe is fundamental. This clarity helps in calculating your net worth and making informed decisions that align with your financial goals.

Importance of Emergency Funds: Having an emergency fund that covers 3-6 months of living expenses provides a safety net during unexpected events, ensuring financial stability and peace of mind.

Power of Investing Early: Starting your investments early leverages the power of compound interest, significantly growing your wealth over time.

Investing is Accessible: Modern technology has made investing accessible to everyone, even with small amounts of capital. Platforms like mutual funds, SIPs, and robo-advisors have democratized the investment landscape.

Saving Alone Isn't Enough: While saving is important, investing is crucial to outpace inflation and grow your wealth. Diversifying your investments is key to a robust financial strategy.

Continuous Learning: Setting regular financial literacy goals, such as reading finance books or attending workshops, is essential for staying informed and making wise financial decisions.

Transforming Limiting Beliefs: Identifying and reframing negative beliefs about money into positive affirmations can transform your financial mindset and open new opportunities for growth.

50/30/20 Rule: Allocating 50% of income to needs, 30% to wants, and 20% to savings and debt repayment offers a balanced approach to managing your finances.

Zero-Based Budgeting: Ensuring that every rupee has a specific role helps in managing expenses effectively and achieving financial goals.

Envelope System: Using physical or digital envelopes to categorize and control spending can prevent overspending and maintain financial discipline.

Budgeting Apps: Utilizing apps like Money View, Goodbudget, and Wallet simplifies the process of tracking expenses, setting goals, and managing budgets efficiently.

Automated Savings: Setting up automatic transfers to savings accounts ensures that saving becomes a consistent habit, building a strong financial foundation without constant effort.

Rule of 72: This rule helps estimate how long it will take for an investment to double at a fixed annual rate of return, aiding in better financial planning.

Balancing Risk and Reward: Understanding the risk-reward relationship is crucial for making informed investment decisions. Diversification and maintaining an emergency fund are essential strategies.

Modern Asset Classes: Including cryptocurrencies and tech stocks in your investment portfolio can enhance diversification and potential returns, reflecting the evolving financial landscape.

Warren Buffett's Value Investing: Investing in undervalued companies with strong fundamentals and holding them long-term can lead to significant financial gains.

Ray Dalio's Diversification: The "All Weather Portfolio" emphasizes spreading investments across uncorrelated assets to reduce risk and achieve stable returns.

Cathie Wood's Innovation Focus: Investing in disruptive technologies like AI, robotics, and blockchain can lead to exponential growth and staying ahead in the market.

Creating a Financial Discipline Plan: Tracking spending, creating a budget, automating savings, and avoiding new debt are steps to build financial discipline.

Delayed Gratification: Applying principles like the Marshmallow Test to finance, such as waiting before making purchases, can improve financial outcomes.

Building a Financial Network: Engaging with financial advisors, successful investors, and industry experts can provide valuable insights and opportunities for growth.

Finding a Mentor: A mentor with relevant experience and aligned goals can accelerate your financial learning and development significantly.

Joining Financial Education Groups: Participating in or starting financial education groups fosters collective learning and support, enhancing your financial knowledge.

Personal Branding: Building a personal brand that reflects your financial expertise and goals can attract opportunities and establish credibility in the financial community.

Gratitude Journaling: Reflecting regularly on financial achievements fosters a sense of progress and satisfaction.

Savoring Financial Milestones: Celebrating financial milestones reinforces positive behaviors and motivates continued progress towards your financial goals.

Keep in mind, chasing wealth is a never-ending adventure filled with lessons, adjustments, and growth. Crafting a financial plan that's all your own is your next big move on this wealth-building journey. Let me walk you through a step-by-step guide designed to integrate the wisdom from this book into your unique financial reality.

Step-by-Step Guide to Applying This Book's Insights to Your Financial Plan

Step 1: Reflect on Key Concepts from the Book

Start by revisiting each chapter and highlighting the core principles that resonated with you the most. Whether it was understanding the difference between assets and liabilities, the importance of investing early, or the strategies for financial discipline, make a list of these key points. Use this list as a foundational guide for building your personalized plan.

Step 2: Assess Your Financial Status

Use the templates and exercises provided in the book to thoroughly assess your current financial status. This includes detailed tracking of your income, expenses, assets, and liabilities. The book's sections on budgeting and financial planning offer methods and tools to help you organize this information effectively.

Step 3: Set Financial Goals Using the Book's Frameworks

With your financial assessment in hand, align your goals with the strategies discussed in the book. For example, if you're influenced by the investment philosophies of Warren Buffett or Ray Dalio, define how you can incorporate their strategies into your own investment goals. Use the SMART criteria model from the book to ensure your goals are well-defined and actionable.

Step 4: Develop a Tailored Action Plan

Based on the book's insights on budgeting methods like the 50/30/20 rule or zero-based budgeting, choose a framework that best suits your lifestyle and financial goals. The book provides specific steps and examples that you can adapt to fit your personal financial situation. Implement these by setting up automated systems for savings and regular check-ins to monitor your progress.

Step 5: Leverage Technology for Efficiency

Integrate the recommended technological tools from the book, such as budgeting apps and investment platforms, to enhance your financial management. These tools are designed to make the tracking and managing of your financial activities more accessible and effective, directly reflecting the book's emphasis on leveraging technology to improve financial outcomes.

Step 6: Apply Behavioral Strategies for Long-Term Success

Incorporate the psychological insights from the book, such as the lessons from the Marshmallow Test on delayed gratification, to improve your financial behaviors. Set up systems that reward your financial discipline, like savings milestones that lead to rewards, to maintain motivation and commitment.

Step 7: Build and Maintain Your Financial Network

Utilize the networking strategies detailed in the book to connect with mentors, join financial education groups, and engage with communities that can provide support and opportunities for growth. Regularly contribute to these networks to establish yourself as a knowledgeable and reliable member of your financial community.

Step 8: Regular Review and Adaptation

Set periodic reviews to assess your financial progress. Use the book's guidelines on revisiting and adjusting your financial plan to adapt to any life changes or financial shifts. This ensures your plan remains relevant and aligned with your evolving financial needs and goals.

Now that we've mapped out how to apply the insights from this book, it's crucial to emphasize the importance of staying informed. In the ever-evolving world of finance, being well-informed is your best defense against risk and your greatest asset for seizing opportunities.

The Importance of Staying Informed

Staying informed is vital for wealth maximization. It empowers you to make informed decisions, identify lucrative opportunities, and mitigate risks effectively. Here's why staying updated is essential:

Identifying Opportunities: Keeping up with financial news allows you to spot emerging trends and capitalize on market movements. This can lead to timely investments in high-growth sectors or assets, significantly boosting your returns.

Risk Management: Being aware of global and local events helps you assess geopolitical risks and their potential impact on your investments. This knowledge enables you to make decisions that minimize risks and protect your financial security.

Informed Decision-Making: Access to up-to-date information ensures that you make well-informed decisions about buying or selling stocks, currencies, or commodities. This reduces the likelihood of poor investment choices based on outdated or incomplete information.

Regulatory Compliance: Staying informed about regulatory changes ensures that you remain compliant with new laws and regulations, avoiding potential legal issues and fines. This is particularly important in the rapidly evolving financial landscape.

Market Awareness: Understanding market dynamics and economic indicators helps you anticipate market movements and adjust your strategies accordingly. This awareness is essential for maintaining a competitive edge in the financial markets.

Here are comprehensive strategies to stay informed:

Traditional News Outlets

Television and Newspapers: Channels like CNN, BBC, and newspapers like The New York Times and Reuters offer in-depth coverage and analysis of major economic events. These sources provide reliable and comprehensive news to help you stay informed about global and local developments.

Daily Newsletters: Subscribe to daily newsletters from reputable news websites to receive the most important financial news directly in your inbox, keeping you updated on the go.

Financial Websites and Portals

Real-Time Updates: Websites like Bloomberg, Reuters, and CNBC provide real-time updates, expert opinions, and a wealth of financial data. These platforms are essential for staying current with market trends and economic indicators.

Customized Alerts: Many financial websites allow you to set up customized alerts for specific stocks, sectors, or economic events. This feature ensures that you receive immediate notifications about relevant news, helping you make timely investment decisions.

Social Media Platforms and Financial Blogs

Twitter and LinkedIn: Follow financial experts, companies, and news outlets on social media platforms like Twitter and LinkedIn for quick access to breaking news and expert analysis. Engaging with these platforms allows for real-time updates and discussions with other investors.

Financial Blogs: Blogs written by financial experts offer in-depth analysis and unique perspectives on market trends and investment strategies. Regularly reading these blogs can enhance your understanding of complex financial topics and keep you informed about niche markets.

News Aggregators

Google News and AP News: These aggregators gather news and financial data from various sources and organize it for easy access. They help discover new online sites and blogs, particularly those focusing on international news and markets, ensuring a broad and comprehensive view of financial developments.

Podcasts and Audio Updates

Financial Podcasts: For those who prefer audio content, financial podcasts provide updates on breaking news and investing trends. Listening to these podcasts during commutes or workouts can keep you informed without taking extra time out of your day.

News Tickers and Brokerage Platforms

News Tickers: Download news ticker programs that run along the top or bottom of your computer screen, allowing for passive monitoring of news headlines while you work on other tasks. Clicking on ticker headlines provides full articles for detailed information.

Brokerage Platforms: Many brokerage platforms offer integrated news feeds and alerts for the stocks and ETFs you follow. These platforms provide a seamless way to stay updated on market movements and investment opportunities.

Regulatory Change Management Frameworks

Cloud-Based Content Platforms: Use cloud-based platforms to track regulatory content from global and regional regulators. These platforms aggregate information from industry associations, national and local media, and specialized content providers, making it easier to manage and analyze regulatory updates.

Proactive Monitoring: Develop a robust regulatory change management framework involving proactive monitoring of regulatory updates and implementing changes promptly. This approach helps you remain compliant and adapt to new regulations efficiently.

This vigilance and proactive approach will ensure that you are always prepared to make the best financial decisions for your future.

Crafting a Personal Manifesto for Financial Wealth and Well-Being

Diving into how we stay informed, it's undeniable that this plays a huge role in navigating our financial world. Keeping up with the latest trends and shifts is as important as making sure our money moves align with our core values and dreams. I want to share a game-changing exercise that's transformed my approach and could do the same for you, helping you pinpoint your financial values, set solid long-term goals, and really get what financial freedom means on a personal level.

Exercise: Articulating Your Financial Blueprint

This exercise is designed to help you reflect deeply on your financial aspirations and what shapes them. By the end of it, you should have a clearer vision of your financial goals aligned with your personal values, enabling you to pursue true financial freedom.

Step 1: Define Your Personal Financial Values

Reflect on Influences: Consider the factors that have shaped your views on money. This might include your upbringing, key life events, or influential people in your life. Write these down.

Identify Core Values: What values matter most to you in life? Honesty, security, independence, or perhaps generosity? Determine which of these values you want to reflect in your financial decisions.

Write a Values Statement: Sum up your financial values in a statement. For example, "I value security and freedom, and my financial decisions must foster both stability and the ability to enjoy life's experiences."

Step 2: Establish Clear Long-Term Financial Goals

Vision for the Future: Imagine your ideal financial scenario in five, ten, or twenty years. What does this picture look like? Are you aiming for early retirement, owning a home, or perhaps funding an education for your children?

Set Specific Goals: Based on your vision, define specific long-term goals. For instance, "Save ₹1,000,000 for a down payment on a home in ten years."

Make It Measurable: Ensure each goal is measurable. How much will you need to save monthly or annually to achieve each goal? Break it down.

Step 3: Define What Financial Freedom Means to You

Personal Definition of Freedom: Financial freedom can mean different things to different people. Does it mean living debt-free, achieving a certain net worth, or having the freedom to work less? Define what it specifically means for you.

Align Freedom with Values and Goals: Ensure that your definition of financial freedom aligns with your values and goals. If independence is a core value, financial freedom might mean having enough passive income to not rely on a 9-to-5 job.

Plan Steps to Achieve Freedom: Outline practical steps to reach this freedom. This could involve investment strategies, career decisions, or lifestyle changes.

Step 4: Regularly Revisit and Revise

Annual Review: Commit to reviewing this exercise annually. As your life circumstances and financial situation evolve, so too may your values, goals, and definition of freedom.

Adjust as Necessary: Be prepared to make adjustments. Flexibility is key to staying aligned with your evolving financial identity.

By taking the time to perform this exercise, you'll align your financial strategies with your deepest values and pave a clearer path toward true financial freedom. This alignment ensures that every financial decision supports a well-defined purpose, empowering you to build a fulfilling and secure financial future.

Appendices

Practical Exercises and Tools for Financial Planning and Investment Analysis

As we approach the final steps of our financial journey, it's essential to arm ourselves with practical exercises and tools that will help us effectively plan and analyze our investments. Here are five tangible exercises and five unique tools that can make a significant difference in your financial planning and investment analysis.

Exercises

Monthly Expense Tracking

Purpose: Gain a clear understanding of your spending habits.

Steps

Collect Data: For one month, track every expense meticulously. Use a spreadsheet, app, or notebook.

Categorize Spending: Divide your expenses into categories such as housing, groceries, utilities, entertainment, and transportation.

Analyze Trends: At the end of the month, review your spending. Identify areas where you can cut back and redirect funds towards savings or investments.

This exercise helps you identify unnecessary expenditures and redirect those funds towards achieving your financial goals.

SMART Goal Setting

Purpose: Set clear, achievable financial goals.

Steps

Specific: Define a clear and specific financial goal (e.g., save ₹100,000 for an emergency fund).

Measurable: Ensure your goal can be tracked and measured (e.g., save ₹10,000 each month).

Achievable: Set a realistic goal considering your income and expenses.

Relevant: Align the goal with your broader financial values and objectives.

Time-bound: Set a deadline for achieving your goal (e.g., within 10 months).

Using the SMART framework helps create actionable and attainable financial objectives.

Debt Repayment Plan

Purpose: Strategize to pay off debt efficiently.

Steps

List Debts: Write down all your debts, including interest rates and minimum payments.

Choose a Strategy: Decide between the debt snowball (paying off the smallest debt first) or debt avalanche (tackling the highest interest rate debt first) methods.

Make a Plan: Allocate extra funds each month towards the chosen debt while making minimum payments on others.

Track Progress: Regularly review and adjust your plan as needed.

A structured debt repayment plan helps you pay off debts faster and save on interest payments.

Investment Portfolio Review

Purpose: Ensure your investment portfolio is balanced and aligned with your goals.

Steps

Assess Current Portfolio: List all your investments, including stocks, bonds, mutual funds, and real estate.

Evaluate Performance: Compare each investment's performance against market benchmarks and your financial goals.

Rebalance: Adjust your portfolio to maintain your desired asset allocation. Consider factors like risk tolerance and time horizon.

Set Review Schedule: Plan to review your portfolio at least annually.

Regularly reviewing and rebalancing your portfolio helps optimize returns and manage risks.

Retirement Savings Checkup

Purpose: Ensure you are on track to meet your retirement goals.

Steps

Calculate Retirement Needs: Estimate how much money you will need for retirement, considering factors like lifestyle, inflation, and life expectancy.

Review Current Savings: Evaluate how much you have saved so far in your retirement accounts.

Identify Gaps: Determine if there is a shortfall between your current savings and future needs.

Adjust Contributions: Increase your monthly contributions to retirement accounts if needed.

Regular checkups ensure you stay on track to achieve a comfortable retirement.

Tools for Financial Planning and Investment Analysis

Personal Capital

Purpose: Investment tracking and retirement planning.

Features: Offers a comprehensive dashboard to track investments, analyze asset allocation, and plan for retirement with its Retirement Planner tool.

Benefit: Helps you monitor and optimize your investment portfolio.

YNAB (You Need A Budget)

Purpose: Budgeting and financial planning.

Features: Emphasizes proactive budgeting by allocating every dollar a job, tracking spending, and adjusting budgets in real-time.

Benefit: Encourages disciplined budgeting and helps break the paycheck-to-paycheck cycle.

Robinhood

Purpose: Commission-free trading and investment management.

Features: Allows users to trade stocks, ETFs, and cryptocurrencies with no commission fees. Provides real-time market data and analysis tools.

Benefit: Makes investing accessible and affordable for beginners and seasoned investors alike.

Morningstar

Purpose: Investment research and analysis.

Features: Offers in-depth research, ratings, and analysis on stocks, mutual funds, ETFs, and market trends.

Benefit: Provides comprehensive data and insights to help you make informed investment decisions.

By incorporating these exercises and tools into your financial routine, you'll be better equipped to plan, manage, and analyze your finances effectively. This proactive approach ensures you stay aligned with your financial goals and adapt to any changes in your financial scenario.

Customizable Templates for Budgeting, Debt Repayment Plans, Investment Analysis, and Retirement Planning

As we delve deeper into the practical aspects of financial management, a crucial tool at your disposal is the Monthly Budget Template. This template is your roadmap to understanding and controlling your finances effectively. It helps you align your spending with your financial goals, ensuring you can save, invest, and reduce debt efficiently.

Monthly Budget Template

The Monthly Budget Template is designed to help you track and manage your monthly income against your expenses comprehensively. It provides a clear visual breakdown of where your money comes from and where it goes, empowering you to make informed financial decisions.

Components of the Template

Income: This section records all your income streams. Whether it's your salary, earnings from freelance projects, or returns on investments, each source is listed to give you a total income overview.

Fixed Expenses: These are your non-negotiable expenses such as rent or mortgage payments, utility bills, insurance premiums, and any loan payments. Tracking these helps ensure you meet your essential commitments without fail.

Variable Expenses: This category varies month by month. It includes groceries, transportation costs, entertainment, and dining out. Monitoring these expenses is key to identifying areas where you can adjust your spending habits if necessary.

Savings and Investments: It's crucial to pay yourself first. This section is for outlining how much you allocate to your emergency fund, retirement savings, and any other investment plans each month.

Debt Repayment: Detailing your credit card payments, personal loans, and student loans here helps you track your progress in debt reduction and manage your payment schedules effectively.

Template Structure

The template is structured to provide clarity and ease of use. Each section is clearly marked, with columns for budgeted amounts, actual amounts spent or received, and the difference between the two. This format allows for meticulous tracking and highlights variances that may need your attention.

Category	Budgeted Amount	Actual Amount	Difference
Income - Salary - Freelance - Investments Total Income			
Fixed Expenses - Rent/Mortgage - Utilities - Insurance - Loan Payments Total Fixed Expenses			

Category	Budgeted Amount	Actual Amount	Difference
Variable Expenses - Groceries - Transportation - Entertainment - Dining Out Total Variable Expenses			
Savings & Investments - Emergency Fund - Retirement - Other Savings Total Savings & Inv.			
Debt Repayment - Credit Cards - Personal Loans - Student Loans Total Debt Repayment			
Total Expenses			
Net Income			

Debt Repayment Plan Template

Purpose: To create a structured plan for paying off debts.

Components

Debt List: All debts with details (creditor, balance, interest rate, minimum payment).

Debt Repayment Strategy: Choose between the debt snowball method (paying off smallest debts first) or the debt avalanche method (paying off highest interest rate debts first).

Monthly Payment Plan: Allocate payments to each debt based on chosen strategy.

Progress Tracking: Monitor payments and remaining balances.

Investment Analysis Template

Purpose: To analyze and report on investment performance and trends.

Components

Investment Summary: Overview of all investments (stocks, bonds, real estate, etc.).

Performance Metrics: ROI, annual growth rate, dividends, etc.

Risk Assessment: Volatility, market conditions, risk factors.

Future Projections: Expected performance based on current trends.

Recommendations: Buy, hold, sell decisions.

Retirement Planning Spreadsheet

Purpose: To plan and track retirement savings and income.

Components

Current Age and Retirement Age: Basic personal information.

Current Savings: Total amount saved for retirement.

Annual Savings: Amount saved each year until retirement.

Expected Rate of Return: Average annual return on investments.

Retirement Income Needs: Estimated annual expenses during retirement.

Additional Income Sources: Social Security, pensions, annuities.

Withdrawal Rate: Percentage of savings withdrawn annually.

Online Calculators for Financial Planning

Reflecting on the practical tools we've explored in the previous section, I want to share another invaluable resource that can simplify your financial planning journey: online calculators. These tools are designed to help you make informed decisions about your finances, whether you're saving for a goal, repaying a loan, or planning for retirement.

I remember when I first started using these calculators. They transformed my approach to financial planning by providing clear, actionable insights that I could rely on. Here's a list of some of the most useful calculators that you can use to fine-tune your financial strategies:

Savings Goal Calculators

These calculators help you figure out how much you need to save to reach your financial goals, whether it's for a vacation, a new car, or an emergency fund.

The Calculator Site

Purpose: Helps you determine how long it will take to save for a goal and how much you need to save each month.

Benefits: Simple and user-friendly, providing quick insights into your savings timeline and monthly targets.

NerdWallet Savings Goal Calculator

Purpose: Calculates how much you need to save each month to reach a specific savings goal.

Benefits: Offers detailed breakdowns and lets you adjust various parameters to see different saving scenarios.

Investor.gov Savings Goal Calculator

Purpose: Provides the monthly contribution amounts needed to reach a savings goal.

Benefits: Ideal for understanding the impact of regular contributions and compound interest over time.

Loan Repayment Calculators

These calculators estimate your monthly payments and help you understand the costs associated with different types of loans.

Bankrate Loan Calculator

Purpose: Estimates monthly payments for various types of loans, including mortgages, auto loans, and personal loans.

Benefits: Provides a comprehensive view of your loan repayments, including interest costs and payment schedules.

Calculator.net Loan Calculator

Purpose: Calculates repayment plans, interest costs, and amortization schedules for different loan types.

Benefits: Offers a detailed analysis of how much you'll pay over the life of the loan and helps you plan your finances better.

Retirement Savings Calculators

These calculators project how much you need to save to ensure a comfortable retirement, taking into account your current savings and future needs.

T. Rowe Price Retirement Income Calculator

Purpose: Projects monthly retirement income and potential shortfalls based on various scenarios.

Benefits: Helps you understand how much you need to save now to meet your retirement income goals and identifies any potential shortfalls.

Groww Retirement Planning Calculator

Purpose: Helps determine the total corpus needed for retirement and the monthly savings required.

Benefits: Provides a clear picture of your retirement savings needs and helps you plan your contributions accordingly.

5 Paisa Retirement Calculator

Purpose: Estimates the retirement fund you can build based on current age, investment amount, and expected return.

Benefits: Allows you to adjust variables to see different retirement outcomes, helping you plan more effectively.

Why Use These Calculators?

Using these calculators can transform the way you approach financial planning. They offer:

Clarity and Precision: By inputting your financial details, you get precise calculations that help you understand exactly where you stand and what you need to do.

Time-Saving: These tools save you from manual calculations, giving you more time to focus on implementing your financial strategies.

Informed Decision-Making: With clear insights, you can make better financial decisions, whether it's saving more each month, adjusting your loan repayments, or increasing your retirement contributions.

I encourage you to explore these calculators and use them regularly as part of your financial planning routine. They are powerful tools that can help you achieve financial stability and success.

Recommended Reading and Resources for Continued Education in Wealth Maximization

As we close the covers of this book, your journey to wealth maximization is just beginning. The real challenge lies in continually applying and expanding upon what you've learned. To aid in this, I've curated a list of exceptional resources that will keep you engaged and informed. These platforms offer fresh perspectives and deep dives into various aspects of personal finance and wealth management.

Financial Blogs and Websites

Jagoinvestor: This resource is a treasure trove for those looking to manage their finances more effectively. From exploring family trusts to understanding macroeconomic trends that impact your investments, Jagoinvestor makes complex topics accessible to everyone.

Safal Niveshak: Here, the focus is on value investing and achieving financial independence. The blog is well-regarded for its clear, actionable advice that simplifies the journey towards financial literacy and independence.

Capitalmind: Whether you're a beginner or a seasoned investor, Capitalmind offers insightful articles that enhance your understanding of personal finance, tax strategies, and sophisticated investment techniques.

StackWealth Blog: This blog addresses common but overlooked topics like portfolio overlap and tax harvesting. It's ideal for those who wish to refine their investment strategies to suit varying market conditions.

Wealth Management Platforms

Third Financial: This platform revolutionizes wealth management by offering comprehensive support to wealth managers and financial advisors, enhancing the efficiency of financial services.

Addepar: For investors seeking detailed data aggregation and analysis, Addepar stands out as a fintech solution that combines robust technology with user-friendly reporting features.

Wealthfront: Perfect for those who prefer a hands-off approach to investing, Wealthfront offers automated investment management that prioritizes personalized financial planning and cost efficiency.

Educational Resources

Slideshare Presentations: Look for presentations like "Profit Maximization vs Wealth Maximization" to get succinct, visually engaging insights into key financial concepts and strategies.

Corporate Finance Institute (CFI): CFI provides comprehensive courses that blend financial theory with practical applications, ideal for those looking to deepen their understanding of financial management.

Intellipaat Blog: This blog discusses the nuances of wealth maximization, providing valuable perspectives on how it can contribute to sustained financial health and stakeholder value.

These resources are communities where you can interact with experts, ask questions, and stay on the cutting edge of financial trends and innovations. Engaging with these platforms will not only reinforce what you've learned but also expose you to new ideas and strategies that can be crucial in navigating the complexities of wealth maximization.

As we close the pages of this journey towards wealth maximization, remember that the path to financial freedom is both enriching and demanding. You've now equipped yourself with the knowledge and tools necessary to tackle the complexities of personal finance and investment strategies. But knowledge alone is not enough—action is the key to transformation.

Take the first step today. Whether it's refining your budget, adjusting your investment portfolio, or expanding your financial network, begin with one action from this book. Commit to applying one principle every month, and track your progress. The road to wealth is paved with persistence and discipline, and every small step is a part of your larger journey towards financial independence. Don't let this book gather dust on your shelf. Revisit it, reflect on the exercises, and continuously adapt your strategies as your financial situation and the external economic world evolve. Share your insights and progress with your community, and keep the cycle of learning and growing alive.Take charge of your financial future now—because if not now, when? If not you, who?

www.ingramcontent.com/pod-product-compliance
Lightning Source LLC
LaVergne TN
LVHW041024150826
845672LV00001B/202

* 9 7 9 8 8 9 4 4 6 3 8 2 7 *